the beauty of believing

# Girl Politics

Friends, Cliques, and Really
Mean Chicks

REVISED EDITION

## Also by Nancy Rue

*You! A Christian Girl's Guide to Growing Up*
*Everyone Tells Me to Be Myself ... but I Don't Know Who I Am*

### Sophie's World Series

*Meet Sophie (Book One)*
*Sophie Steps Up (Book Two)*
*Sophie and Friends (Book Three)*
*Sophie's Friendship Fiasco (Book Four)*
*Sophie Flakes Out (Book Five)*
*Sophie's Drama (Book Six)*

### The Lucy Series

*Lucy Doesn't Wear Pink (Book One)*
*Lucy Out of Bounds (Book Two)*
*Lucy's Perfect Summer (Book Three)*
*Lucy Finds Her Way (Book Four)*

## Other books in the growing Faithgirlz!™ library

### Bibles

*The Faithgirlz! Bible*
*NIV Faithgirlz! Backpack Bible*

### Faithgirlz! Bible Studies

*Secret Power of Love*
*Secret Power of Joy*
*Secret Power of Goodness*
*Secret Power of Grace*

**Check out www.faithgirlz.com**

the beauty of believing

# Girl Politics

## Friends, Cliques, and Really Mean Chicks

Nancy
Rue

REVISED EDITION

ZONDERVAN®

ZONDERVAN.com/
AUTHORTRACKER
*follow your favorite authors*

So we fix our eyes not on what is seen, but what is unseen.
For what is seen is temporary, but what is unseen is eternal.

2 Corinthians 4:18

ZONDERKIDZ

*Girl Politics*

Copyright © 2007, 2013 by Nancy Rue

This title is also available as a Zondervan ebook.
Visit www.zondervan.com/ebooks

Requests for information should be addressed to:
Zonderkidz, 5300 Patterson Ave. SE, Grand Rapids, Michigan 49530

Library of Congress Cataloging-in-Publication Data

Rue, Nancy.
    Girl politics : friends, cliques, and really mean chicks / Nancy Rue. — Updated ed.
      p. cm. — (Faithgirlz!)
      ISBN 978-0-310-73321-8 (softcover)
    1. Female friendship—Juvenile literature. 2. Friendship—Juvenile literature. 3. Bullying
in schools—Juvenile literature. 4. Christian life—Juvenile literature. I. Title.
      BF575.F66R84 2013
241'.676208342--dc23                                                            2012041249

Published in association with the literary agency of Alive Communications, Inc., 7680 Goddard Street, Suite 200, Colorado Springs, CO 80920. www.alivecommunications.com

Zonderkidz is a trademark of Zondervan.

*Interior design: Sarah Molegraaf*
*Art direction and cover design: Kris Nelson and Jody Langley*

*Printed in the United States of America*

HB 09.25.2017

# Contents

# How to Read This Book

This book is jam-packed full with lots of info to help you. Here's what you can expect:

## HERE'S THE DEAL

Tons of information about why friendship stuff happens and what you can do about it. This always comes from questions mini-women have asked me.

## That Is SO Me

Quizzes to help you figure out where you are on things like BFFs and bullying and cliques. These are the kind of tests you don't have to study for! And no grades!

- - - - - - - - - - - - - - - - - - - - - - - - - - - - - - - - - - -

## GOT GOD?

What God says about friendship and the way we need to treat other people. You'll be surprised what the Bible says about YOUR life.

## YOU CAN DO IT

An artsy-craftsy way for you to try out what you've read about. And not just you, but you AND your friends. (That only makes sense, right?)

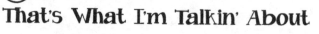

## That's What I'm Talkin' About

A place for you to fill in some blanks about your own friend-ship stuff—or draw or doodle—or even journal if you really like to write and write and … write

## *Mini-Women Say*

66 Quotes from tween girls like you who say some things so much better than I can. 99

## Just So You Know

Fun facts to make you feel smarter. (They're good things to talk about when you want to steer the con-versation away from gossip!)

## Who, ME?

Things you can do super fast to help you see how all this friend-information fits YOU.

Let's get started!

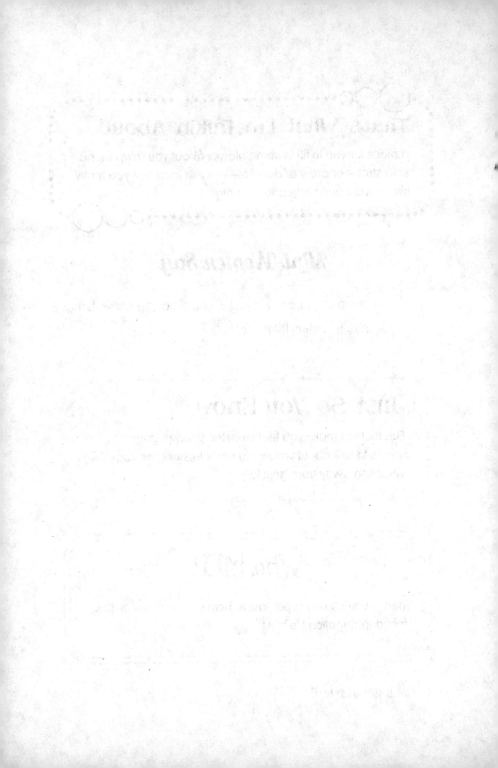

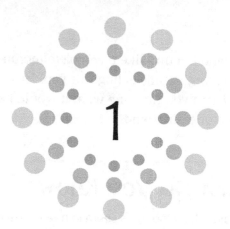

1

# Why Can't We All Just Get Along?

You are a mini-woman.

That means you're no longer that sweet little baby girl-friend who plays with the other baby girlfriends her mom picks out and doesn't care who they are as long as they don't take the red crayon when she's using it.

It also means you haven't yet lost your mind and become a teenager who might ditch her BFF for the same guy you both thought was an annoying boy creature back when you were twelve—when you were mini-women, and therefore sane.

You are a mini-woman, which means you *get* that girl-friends are more important than the picture you're coloring or the boy who's acting like a complete moron to get your attention. Having friends is huge for you. Huge.

Seriously, can you imagine what it would be like not to have at least one girlfriend?

## Just So You Know

Studies show that girls seem to need close friendships more than boys do.

What would you *do*—

- at lunchtime?

- at recess (because who plays on the swings anymore)?

- when something freaky happened to you?

- when something incredibly cool happened to you?

- when you were bored out of your skull?

- when your feelings were hurt and you ran to the bathroom crying?

- when you needed to know that very minute you were okay just like you are?

And how would you *feel* if you didn't have at least one friend?

# Who, ME?

Circle the feelings YOU have had when you were friendless (even just for one day).

Ugly    Scared    Anxious    Sad    Lonely    Freaked-Out    Bored    Hurt    Confused    Lost    Depressed    Angry

Whether you can't even imagine it or you're living it right now (ugh), it's not a news flash to you that having friends is mega-important.

It's just that it's not always easy.

No matter how much you love your BFF or your CFFs (that's Close Friends Forever), sometimes you're just not going to get along. (Ya think?)

You *can* make up and go, "What were we even fighting about?" ... but sometimes you don't.

Girls who don't even *like* you can get involved.

A girl, or a whole group of girls, can decide that making you miserable is their new career.

You might end up in a situation where there isn't a friend in sight.

66 I had been really good friends with Megan since second grade. We did everything together. But in fourth grade, Nikki came to school. At first we all three got along, but then Megan and Nikki started getting together and having sleepovers and doing everything without including me. I was really depressed and discouraged. I still tried to be nice to both of them, but it was hard. I got mad one day and asked them why they weren't including me in any of their activities. They didn't really say anything. We didn't talk to each other for a long time. 99

Even if none of that has happened to you, it could, or you'll at least know somebody who has had to go through it. Girl politics are happening all over the tween years (and they always have).

That's why you have this book in your hand right now. I've written it to help you—

- know what REAL friendship looks like (and doesn't look like!).

- fix the "Friendship Flubs" everybody makes because you're, uh, human.

- stay away from the major mistakes like cliques and bullying.

- be a part of making your girl community a place where every girl can be the true self she was made to be.

And just so you know, I've had a lot of help with this book from mini-women who, like you, are making their way through girl politics this very moment. You'll see their totally true stories here, and you'll know you are SO not alone.

## Just So You Know

People who have studied this stuff say girls get more upset than boys do when they have problems with their friends.

Some of my mini-women friends shared their thoughts with me about what makes a true friend. Here's what they said:

- A real friend is a person who sticks with you no matter what, even if another friend comes along.

- A true friend knows you're completely INSANE and loves you anyway.

- A true friend is someone to cry with you when you're hiding out in the bathroom.

- A true BFF loves you more than things.

- A real friend will tell you the truth, even if it hurts.

- A true friend is like family, better than a sister.

- Somebody who is your real friend knows you right down to what you like as pizza toppings.

- For me, a BFF is somebody you don't have to put on an act around.

- A true friend is one who has your back and won't leave you when you're not cool.

66 Why is having friends such a big deal now? When I was little, it didn't matter that much because I was all about my family, but now, like if my BFF is absent from school, I'm totally lost! 99

## HERE'S THE DEAL

It's way normal to want close friends and to be completely bummed out if you don't have them or if things don't go that well when you do. Having best buds helps you get some skills you're going to need your whole life:

- Treating people right so they'll love you when they don't **have** to (like your family does).

- Feeling safe with people outside your own family.

- Knowing what kind of people you want to hang out with—and what kind aren't good for you.

- Discovering what you're like when things don't go the way you want.

- Figuring out how to settle arguments or not have them every ten minutes.

That's why it's not only fun, but it's also important to have friends!

66 Your best friend just gets you. 99

**66** She loves you when you're hurt emotionally, even if being hurt makes her hurt too. **99**

**66** She's somebody who gives you warmth when you're in a bad mood. **99**

---

# Who, ME?

Write YOUR definition of a true friend.

_____

_____

_____

_____

_____

---

**66** A true friend will help you when you're doing the wrong thing and need direction. **99**

**66** If my best friend and I have fights and stuff, does that mean we aren't really best friends? **99**

# Who, ME?

Check off the things on the below list that have happened to YOU.

No relationship is perfect. (Have you noticed?) Certain things go down in every friendship and girl group:

○ A girl is accidentally left out.

○ An old friend kind of drifts away to other friends or activities.

○ Arguments and splits happen, and then everybody gets back together (sometimes within the same hour!).

○ Feelings get hurt without anybody meaning for it to happen, like name-calling for fun.

○ People sometimes get jealous.

○ Friends get annoyed with each other. (Imagine that!)

○ A girl doesn't fit into one group for some reason, so she finds another one.

○ You realize a friendship is bad for you, and you have to break it off. (Don't you hate that?)

That's all normal stuff. It's *hard* normal stuff, but it gives you a chance to learn how to work things out with people. We'll talk about those "Friendship Flubs" in chapter 3.

## Just So You Know

Girls who surround themselves with good friends are less likely to be bullied.

Sometimes, though, the things that go on between girls aren't "just a normal part of growing up." No matter what some people might tell you, there are things said and done on purpose to make a girl feel really horrible about herself.

- You can't sit here. This seat's taken.

- Didn't you already wear that outfit this week?

- I'm gonna tell her she can't come to my sleepover after all. I just don't like her anymore.

- My mom's making me invite her, but we're all going to ditch her the whole time.

- Haven't you ever heard of deodorant?

- If you keep hanging out with her, none of us will be your friends anymore.

- I heard—from somebody who totally knows— that she's already kissed a guy.

- Hey, girls, look who ate an entire village this summer!

# Who, ME?

What bullying thing has been said to YOU? Or (gulp) what bullying thing have YOU said to somebody else?

_____

_____

_____

_____

_____

When a girl says or does things like that—on purpose—to take away another girl's power to be herself—and she does it on a regular basis (like, it's practically her job)—that's _bullying_. It _isn't_ normal, and it's definitely not part of real friendship. I'll talk a lot about girl bullying later (like all of chapter 5), but for now, what does a _good_ girl-to-girl relationship look like? How about we start with checking out yours?

# That Is SO Me

Read each sentence beginning below, and then circle the sentence *ending* that's most true for you. It's pretty obvious which one is the "right" answer, but if you pick that one when it isn't true for you, that won't help you a whole bunch. Be really, really honest so you can get all the help you need.

**1. I'm honest with my friend ...**

_____ a. no matter what.

_____ b. unless she might think I'm lame if I tell her the truth.

_____ c. unless I know she'll get mad at me if I say what I really think.

_____ d. only when I'm mad at her.

**2. When my friend and I have problems, I ...**

_____ a. always talk to her about them.

_____ b. figure it's probably my fault and try to fix myself.

_____ c. don't bring it up because she might not be my friend anymore.

_____ d. tell other people what she's doing that I can't stand.

**3. When my friend and I are WAY getting along, I ...**

_____ a. tell her how cool she is.

_____ b. smile to myself and hope it keeps up.

_____ c. don't say anything because I might jinx it.

_____ d. tell her this is the way it has to be all the time or I'm out of there.

**4. When my friend has something to tell me, I ...**

_____ a. listen.

_____ b. think about what I'm going to say when she's through that's just as cool.

_____ c. don't say anything while she's talking, because she'd cut me off anyway.

_____ d. listen until it starts driving me nuts.

**5. When my friend is upset, I ...**

_____ a. do what she needs me to do so she'll feel better.

_____ b. am always afraid I'm going to say something stupid.

_____ c. agree with whatever she says so she won't get upset at _me_.

_____ d. give her advice as soon as I get what she's talking about (or she'll go on for days).

**6. If someone's being mean to my friend, I ...**

_____ a. stand up for her.

_____ b. tell her I would never be mean to her.

_____ c. be extra careful not to be mean myself.

_____ d. take care of it for her because she's kind of a wimp.

**7. If something way cool happens to me, I ...**

_____ a. can't wait to tell my friend because it's even cooler when she squeals with me.

_____ b. wonder if my friend is going to think it's as cool as I do.

_____ c. try not to make it sound as cool as it is so my friend doesn't get jealous that it didn't happen to her.

_____ d. tell my friend right away because she's always trying to be cooler than me (and I hate that).

**8. If my friend tells me a secret and I promise not to tell, I ...**

_____ a. keep it to myself because she trusts me.

_____ b. only tell people I trust.

_____ c. don't tell because if she found out, she would hate me forever.

_____ d. only tell other people if she makes me mad.

## 9. When my friend does something, well, lame, I ...

_____ a. laugh with her so she doesn't feel stupid.

_____ b. wait to see how she feels about it and then do the same (laugh, cry, hide my head in a bag).

_____ c. pretend I didn't notice so she doesn't take her embarrassment out on me.

_____ d. laugh my head off because she's such a klutz all the time!

## 10. I think my friend will always be there ...

_____ a. because we treat each other super well.

_____ b. if I can be as cool as she is.

_____ c. if she doesn't get mad at me.

_____ d. because she knows she needs me.

You were totally and completely honest, right? Even where you realized you aren't the best friend in the world sometimes? Good, because now you really get to understand some things about yourself and your friendships.

Write the letter for the answer you gave to each of the questions next to the number of the question. (You'll notice that they're in groups instead of in order.)

### When it comes to honesty

_____ 1

_____ 2

**Speaking of respect**

_____ 4

_____ 8

**Being supportive or not**

_____ 5

_____ 6

**The whole sharing thing**

_____ 3

_____ 7

**And, of course, the trust issue**

_____ 9

_____ 10

**Look at your A answers**. They tell you where you're the kind of friend every girl wants for her BFF. Keep it up in those areas!

**Then check out your B answers**. Those show you where you kind of let your friend make the decisions about your friendship. It's good to think about other people's feelings, but you have to be true to you too. This book will help you feel more confident about that, and you'll find out you don't have to give in on everything to keep a good friend.

**Now, about those C answers**. These are the ones that help you see when you're sort of, well, afraid of your friend. Will she be mad at you? Will she think you're stupid? Will she get jealous? Will she dump you? In a real friendship, both girls are equal. You'll be able to work on those things with your BFF or discover you can find other friends who don't expect you to tiptoe around them.

**Finally, think about your D answers if you had any**. They mean that in those friendship areas, you don't really respect your BFF and you might be hurting her without even knowing it. Nobody gets to be the boss of the friendship. Right here in *Girl Politics*, you can learn how to be your strong, confident self without walking on your friend. Once you do, your friendship will rock.

## Just So You Know

Girls' fights with friends average an hour in length. Boys? Under five minutes!

# GOT GOD?

Jesus obviously believed in having great friends because he hung around with twelve of his for three straight years, not to mention all the other people he befriended along the way: Mary Magdalene; Mary, Martha, and Lazarus from Bethany; Nicodemus; Zacchaeus. The list goes on.

Jesus didn't just party at weddings and go on boat rides

with them. He was constantly talking to them about how to treat each other. Things like:

> You're blessed when you care. At the moment of being "care-full," you find yourselves cared for.
>
> Matthew 5:7 (The Message)

> If you enter your place of worship and, about to make an offering, you suddenly remember a grudge a friend has against you, abandon your offering, leave immediately, go to this friend and make things right.
>
> Matthew 5:23–24 (The Message)

> Ask yourself what you want people to do for you, then … do it for them.
>
> Matthew 7:12 (The Message)

Those are just a few of the verses. Who knew the Bible could be your total guide to all the stuff that goes on with girls?

• • • • • • • • • • • • • • • • • • • • • • • • • • • • • • • •

Take the passage from 1 Corinthians 13. You mostly hear it at weddings, but Paul (who wrote it in a letter) was talking about friendship love too. If you replace the word *love* with *friendship*, you get this amazing list of the things a rockin' girlfriend relationship should be.

## True friendship

- *never gives up.*
  Work things out, and hang in there.

- *cares more for others than for self.*
  Say what you need, but find out what your BFF needs too.

- *doesn't want what it doesn't have.*
  Don't do a personality makeover on your friend so she'll be how you want her to be.

- *doesn't strut, doesn't have a swelled head, doesn't force itself on others, isn't always "me first."*
  Nobody's the boss.

- *doesn't fly off the handle.*
  You can get annoyed without pitching a wall-eyed hissy fit. Talk things out.

- *doesn't keep score of the sins of others.*
  Forgive mistakes, fix what's wrong, and move on. Enough with the pouting, already.

- *doesn't revel when others grovel.*
  Making your friend feel like a loser is *not* okay. Ever.

- *takes pleasure in the flowering of truth.*
  Who cares who's right and who's wrong? Settle the argument, and get back to the fun.

- *trusts God always.*
  Pray together and for each other. Talk about what God wants you to do.

- *always looks for the best.*
  See the best stuff in each other, and say it. Out loud. A lot.

That's what a true friendship looks like. If that doesn't

describe yours right now, don't decide you're a loser. Just get ready to find out how you can get there.

## Who, ME?

Of all those verses, which one practically stands up and says, "Hey, this is about YOU"?

Put a big ol' star by that one.

## YOU CAN DO IT

### Best Buds Book

Since this book is about getting along with *other girls*, it's a no-brainer that you won't learn the most from it by doing it all by yourself. Hopefully your BFF or your group of close buds will want to learn with you. This section at the end of each chapter shows you a way to share this book with her or them.

Don't have close girlfriends? Just moved to a new town or school, or none of your old girlfriends is in your class anymore? Or are you maybe a bit of a loner or have had trouble finding girls you really want to connect with?

No worries. In fact, you can skip to chapter 4 and read that if you want. Or just think of at least one person you know that you'd like to spend time with (but not somebody who has already dissed you and will of course be missing out on being friends with a great person). Ask her if she'd like to do this activity with you. How cool is that, really, to grow a brand-new friendship from the beginning? Take it step by step. God's in the middle of it with you.

If there really isn't anyone you can work with right now, it's perfectly okay to do this solo. It'll be great preparation for the new friendships that are right around the corner.

## What you'll need:

○ Your best friend, your small group of close friends (not, like, every girl in your whole class!), or one or two girls you'd like to be friends with. (Or just wonderful you!)

○ This book. It would be neat if you all had your own copies, but sharing is fun too.

○ Something you can use to *make* a book. (A three-ring binder, spiral notebook, scrapbook, blank journal, or just some paper stapled between two pieces of construction paper.) You can either make one book together for the whole group, or each girl can make her own, as long as you're working on them at the same time.

○ Fun pens or markers and any other art supplies you and your friends already have on hand.

○ A place to get together where you can all write and draw—like a table or snack bar or the floor of your room—and where you won't be interrupted while you're doing important friend work. Ask your mom to help with that part if you have brothers and sisters (rather than locking them in the closet yourself).

○ Snacks you think your friends will dig. Jesus was always eating with people; it brings people together in a delicious way.

## What you're doing:

Throughout this book, you'll be making your *own* book with your BFF or CFFs that will show you what's already awesome about your friendship and help you make it even more fabulous.

I'm calling it the Best Buds Book (BBB) here, but you'll be giving yours a title that matches your own unique pair or group. At the end of each chapter, I'll give suggestions for adding to your BBB, and of course you'll want to come up with your own ideas on top of that. There is no "right" or "wrong" way to do this.

## How to make it happen:

1. Ask if your friends want to have an even better friendship than you already have—or if they'd like to start a friendship with you. The answer will probably be yes. Who doesn't want that, right?

2. Decide what you're going to call your friendship. In the Sophie Series, she and her friends named themselves the Corn Flakes. Lucy and her pals, in the Lucy novels, called their team the Dreams. See if you can come up with something that describes the biggest thing you have in common, since each of you is a unique individual.

3. One great way to do that is to look at the "Got God?" section to see if a Bible verse helps.

4. Create a "logo": the name and a picture that says what your group is about in one glance. Think about the logos for McDonald's and Nike and even Zonderkidz to see how a logo works.

5. Choose a Bible verse that fits your friendship. Again, the "Got God?" section may help.

6. Put that logo and your Bible verse on the front of your BBB. This is totally the fun part, so go crazy with the art supplies.

7. Then go to work creating the first section of your BBB: What's a True Friend?

8. Look at what other mini-women say about true friends on pages 16 and 17.

9. Make a list of five to ten definitions of true friends that you agree on. Feel free to use quotes from some of the mini-women on pages 16 and 17.

10. Create a beautiful copy of your definitions (like, so gorgeous you could actually frame it) to put in your BBB. This is the kind of friendship you're going to try to live up to from now on.

11. Keep that book (or everybody's books) in a safe place so you can add more at the end of the next chapter. In fact, plan now for getting together again.

# That's What I'm Talkin' About

Here are some things you can fill in or journal about or even draw when you and God are alone and talkin'.

The best thing about when we got together was _____

_____

_____ .

The hardest thing about when we got together was

_____

_____ .

When I think about the times ahead with my friend/friends,

I feel _____

_____

_____ .

I hope _____

_____ .

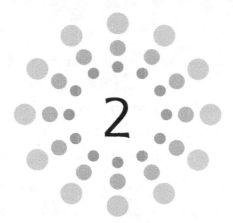

# Closed Cliques ... or Sister Chicks?

One of your fellow mini-women told me this story about something that happened to her. I've changed the names and some of the details (as I'll always do) just so she can stay private, but the experience itself is totally true.

> I go to a girls' group at my church, and there is this girl there: Megi. That isn't her real name. I made it up from the first two letters in MEan and GIrl. Megi is the leader of the clique in our girls' group. She isn't really the "mean that says it to your face" type of person,

but she says mean things about people to her fellow clique-y chicks. I know she does that because when I was new in the group I wanted to be friends with everyone so I wouldn't be by myself, and she told me some mean things about girls in the group.

"One night we went to a sleepover and she was all like, 'Okay, so you have got to sleep next to me tonight. We are going to have soooo much fun together.' So I set up all my things next to her air mattress. When it was forty minutes 'til lights out, she started looking at my bed and trying to move it without me noticing. But I noticed! I asked her what was the matter, and she told me that she wanted me to move because she wanted someone else to sleep next to her, not me.

"I called my mom to come get me, and I cried the whole way home because what type of friend treats another friend the way she treated me?! Since then I've seen her do that to girls over and over, except for the ones she keeps in her clique. What is UP with that?**"**

Yeah, what *is* that about?

It's about the difference between a **clique** and a group of **real friends**. Let's start by seeing what that looks like in your life.

## Just So You Know

*Clique* (pronounced "klik") comes from the French word *coterie,* which means a close, very exclusive, and select group of members. A pretty word for something that usually isn't!

# That Is SO Me

Look at the list of things girl groups do. Then put a big ol' STAR ☆ under the heading that best describes your group: "Not in a Million Years," "Okay, Sometimes," or "Totally."

Remember to be completely honest. After all, nobody's friendships are perfect, right? The more up front you are, the more this chapter can help you to have true CFFs. (That's Close Friends Forever.)

| In my friend group, we: | Not in a Million Years | Okay, Sometimes | Totally |
|---|---|---|---|
| push a girl out if we get sick of her. | | | |
| stick together against the rest of the world. | | | |
| invite another girl in ONLY if she's exactly like us. | | | |

| | Not in a Million Years | Okay, Sometimes | Totally |
|---|---|---|---|
| have rules we follow to stay in the group. | | | |
| have a leader who's in charge. | | | |
| have fights then get back together. | | | |
| take sides among ourselves. | | | |
| show weird people how weird they are. | | | |
| decide what's cool to do, wear, and say—and all do, wear, and say those things. | | | |
| have a lunch table nobody but us sits at. | | | |
| run things at our school, class, youth group, etc. | | | |
| say whatever we want about people. | | | |
| **Now count the stars in each column.** | | | |

(It's okay to photocopy the quiz so everybody can see it at the same time.)

## Not In a Million Years

If most of your stars are in the "Not in a Million Years" column, you definitely have more of a sisterhood than a clique. Keep reading this chapter so you can make absolutely certain you never enter closed clique-dom. You'll want to pay special attention to the stars you put in other columns.

## Okay, Sometimes

If most of your stars are in the "Okay, Sometimes" column, your group of best buds qualifies as a healthy sisterhood ... most of the time. But like all friends, you do have things you could be doing that are way nicer and more open to the girls you aren't as close to. This chapter will help you move right into the Sister Chick column.

## Totally

If most of your stars are in the "Totally" column, you and your friends may have moved into clique-hood, which means you're probably missing out on a lot. You could be hurting other people outside your group, maybe without even knowing it. Read this chapter really carefully, and be ready for some changes that will make you, your girlfriends, and the other girls you know a whole lot happier.

## HERE'S THE DEAL ABOUT CLIQUES

### What a clique is:

When a group of girls gets to be like a closed club that has no room for anybody new, that's a **clique**. It's usually led by one girl who puts herself in charge of deciding who's in and who's out and what's cool and what's not. You can spot a clique by looking for these kinds of things:

- It acts like it's a better friend group than any other friend group (lots of curled lips and rolling eyes).

- The girls in it think they're cool only if they're accepted by the other girls in the group (and are no longer cool if they're shoved out of the group).

- A girl has to earn her way in. (There's no application form, but it sure seems like there must be!)

- And she can be kicked out at any time, sometimes for no reason.

It seems like nobody would want to be part of something like that, but it happens all the time.

## What it LOOKS like:

"My best friends befriended a new girl, which I didn't mind. But when they started doing things with her, they suddenly decided that there could only be three of them. I was booted out and excluded. They put me down all the time. I felt horrible, but somehow numbed myself from the pain. I spent a year as a loner."

"When I started gymnastics, I had no friends there at all. I knew no one, but everyone knew each other, and they acted like I wasn't even there. There was this clique of girls, and one of them was nice to me when her friends weren't around, but when they were, she was totally mean to me. When we went to meets, I ate lunch by myself. I was very sad."

"Now that I think about it, my friends and I were in a clique together. We didn't really exclude anyone because no one ever asked to join. We mostly did what one girl in our group said and wanted, I think because she threatened to leave us and start another group. Now I wonder why we didn't say, 'So go ahead!'"

## What a clique SOUNDS like:

Nicole: Do you guys mind if I sit at your table?
Michelle: Actually, this is a private table.
Michelle's Friend: There's no room anyway.
Nicole: This chair's empty.
Michelle's Other Friend: No, she means there's no room for YOU.
Michelle: No offense, but are you, like, slow or something? We already told you this on the bus ... at recess ...
Michelle's Friend: Are you special ed?
Michelle's Other Friend: (giggle, giggle)

❝True friends don't shun you when a new girl comes in."

"Two girls in my co-op say hi to me and then talk to

each other and forget about me. They don't do it on purpose, but it still hurts."

"When my friends rejected me, I had no one to turn to. It felt HORRIBLE. I felt as if no one wanted me anywhere I went."

"One day I walked up to some of the popular kids and asked if I could hang out with them. They totally snubbed me and tossed their hair as a show of power and walked away. ""

A clique isn't a healthy friend group. It's not Close Friends Forever. A group of really good buds:

- ○ is based on actually *liking* each other (imagine that!) and enjoying some of the same things.

- ○ is always open to new people being friends with them without having to "get rid" of someone to make room for her.

- ○ doesn't label other girls (Geek, Retard, Brainiac) but finds out who they really are.

## So ... why?

"" Maybe it's because I never get included in the popular clique, but seriously, I don't get why anybody would want to be in one. ""

A lot of the cliques you're going to come across *are* made up of "popular" girls that everyone else either likes or wants to copy. Being close to the cool girls makes *them* feel cool too.

If a clique has made being mean to other girls what they're all about, some girls will do anything to work their way in to protect themselves from being the next target for meanness. (We'll talk more about that in chapter 5.)

Let's face it, a clique can look totally fun from the outside: a group of girls always together, knowing where they belong all the time, and being secure that there will always be somebody there. But once they're "in," some girls will stop acting like themselves and try to be more like the other girls in the clique, just to hold on to that safety they think they have there. The thing is, it *isn't* safe. If they make one "mistake," they're outta there.

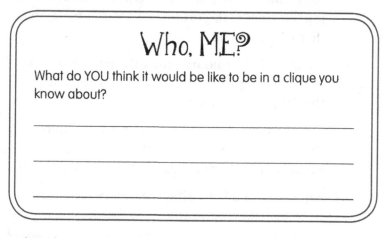

## Who, ME?

What do YOU think it would be like to be in a clique you know about?

_____

_____

_____

## What happens with cliques:

The girls on the OUTSIDE:

○ are like bull's-eyes for teasing and excluding and

rumor-spreading—the really hurtful stuff cliques sometimes do.

- ○ can feel like they're not worth as much (especially when a clique-type girl is all like, "Do I have to work with *her*?").

- ○ are often excluded from parties and sleepovers, just because they aren't "in."

- ○ may get so hurt they start being mean themselves, giving out the same kind of cruelty that's being thrown in their faces.

The girls on the INSIDE:

- ○ can start thinking they really *are* better than everyone else.

- ○ sometimes bully the "outsiders" just to keep feeling like they're important. (We'll talk more about that in chapter 5.)

- ○ are closed off from making any new friends who aren't willing to be exactly like them (down to the filling in their sandwich!).

- ○ aren't allowed to make their own choices in things like clothes or after-school activities because they're afraid *they'll* become "outsiders."

- ○ can be so afraid of losing their place in the clique, they feel they can't afford to be decent to less "popular" kids.

- ○ may not be happy. There can be so much drama in the clique that it gets crazy; her friends don't make her happy—they just make her feel "in." For now.

66 Are ALL popular girls automatically in cliques? Aren't any of them nice? 99

We need to be really careful not to assume that just because a girl is "popular," she must be a total snob, or that a group of friends everybody likes are naturally a mean clique. Check out that popular girl by asking yourself:

○ Is she fun to be around?

○ Does she talk to everybody?

○ Do people feel good when they're around her?

○ Is she understanding when somebody has a problem?

○ Can she be in charge of a project without being bossy?

○ Does she seem comfortable no matter what's going on?

If the answer is yes to those, that's why everyone likes her. If you smile at her and ask open questions like, "Where did you get those cute flip-flops?" and are your fun self around her, she isn't going to say, "Why are you even talking to me?" Who knows? You might get to be buds, even if you aren't in her circle of closest friends.

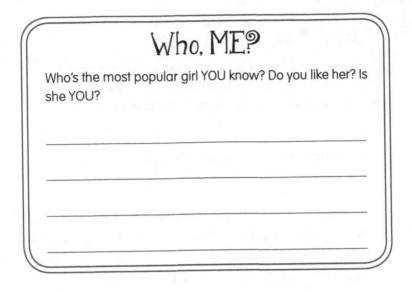

## Who, ME?

Who's the most popular girl YOU know? Do you like her? Is she YOU?

_____

_____

_____

_____

> I see cliques that aren't "the popular kids." Are they okay to be in?

Girls mostly form friend groups because they have things in common, right? They're all in gymnastics, or they belong to the same church, or they share a thing for *Anne of Green Gables*. That's what brings people together.

But if those same groups act the way a clique does—somebody's the boss, there are "rules" or you get kicked out, other girls are considered outsiders and have to be put down and made fun of—it's not healthy or fun.

It's okay to be The Artsy Girls or even The Jesus Freaks as long as you can each be who you are and you don't make anybody else's life miserable.

Before we talk about what to *do* about the Clique Trick, let's see what God has to say about it. That's always the best place to start anyway.

# GOT GOD?

Jesus was definitely popular. Ya think? People climbed trees, hiked up mountains, and had themselves lowered through roofs to be near him.

But Jesus and his disciples weren't a clique, even though they were his best friends and he was clearly the leader.

Unlike the leader of clique, he was all *about* the "outsiders":

- the leper he healed, who was the worst outcast you could imagine (Matthew 8:1–4)

- people who were possessed by demons—not the people most often invited to parties! (Matthew 8:16, 28–32)

- a woman who'd been married a bajillion (okay, five) times and whom no popular guy would even speak to (John 4:1–30)

- little kids, in spite of the disciples trying to run them off (Matthew 19:13–15)

Jesus even associated with those people right in front of the Pharisees.

Now the Pharisees, they were a clique. Jesus warned his disciples about even being around them because the Pharisees loaded people down with rules they couldn't possibly keep all the time. He told them not to let people be experts over their lives but, instead, to save that job for God (Luke 12:4–5).

Although the Pharisees were what we would call a

clique, Jesus didn't lead his friends in some plan to get back at them when he heard they were talking smack about him (Matthew 15:12–14). In fact he was totally real with the Pharisees every time he talked to them (Luke 14:1–24).

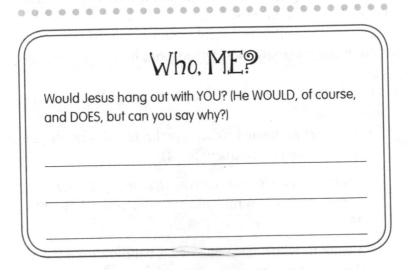

# Who, ME?

Would Jesus hang out with YOU? (He WOULD, of course, and DOES, but can you say why?)

_____

_____

_____

If we're going to be followers of Christ, we need to try to be as much like Jesus as we can, especially when it comes to friends and cliques. You've seen how *he* handled it. Now let's look at what you can do to stay out of cliquedom and have a real sisterhood.

## Just So You Know

Some "popular" girls say they're under a lot of pressure to look perfect and can never have an "off" day. They get exhausted trying to juggle so many friendships and be in charge of so many people. It's not as wonderful as it seems.

## HERE'S THE DEAL ABOUT AVOIDING CLIQUE-DOM

66 How do I keep my group of friends from being a clique? 99

Take the word *popular* out of your vocabulary. It's not about everybody wanting to be with you. It's about you wanting to be with each other.

Do fun stuff together that you all like to do (sleepovers, pizza and movie marathons, making up plays, practicing cartwheels), but let it be okay for everybody to dress and talk how they want to and have other activities besides the ones you do as a group. Go to one friend's soccer games and another one's dance recital and another one's display at the science fair—and celebrate all of it!

If one girl starts to act like she's the boss of all of you, remind her that there's no queen bee. You're all equals.

Never threaten to kick someone out because she doesn't do absolutely everything the group tells her to. There's a huge difference between being kind of alike and having to be identical twins, triplets, or quadruplets. (Even *they* have different personalities and fave colors and pizza preferences.)

Totally refuse to gossip about other girls, especially the girls in a clique. If you bad-mouth them, how are you any different from them?

Make room for new friends who might come along. Invite girls who look lonely to eat at your lunch table. Include the new girl, even though you and your friends feel like your friend slots are all filled. Take a big ol' breath and smile at clique members and at least be polite (as in, no eye rolling or silent treatment). They're probably really great girls inside there somewhere. They're just a little confused right now.

## Just So You Know

Many girls think if they were thinner, they would have more friends and wouldn't be picked on by the clique. They're wrong! Real friends don't care about your weight.

## What a great friend group LOOKS like:

"I spent a whole year outside the 'in' group. I was totally alone, until I found a girl who would accept me. Then we found another girl. We're always happy for each other, and we listen to each other. When one of us isn't around, the other two will e-mail her and say, 'Hey, hiding-out-in-a-ghost-town, are you OK?'"

"My friends and I can tell each other anything and know we can trust that it won't go any further. We borrow each other's books, and we lean on each other when it's hard to stand alone."

"We're like the Three Musketeers (whoever they are!). We don't judge each other because everybody makes mistakes sometimes. We don't say, 'You have to have a boyfriend to be cool.' I guess we just love each other through everything. **99**

## Who, ME?

Okay, first thing that comes to YOUR mind: the best thing about my friends and me is ...

_____

_____

_____

_____

## What a great friend group SOUNDS like:

Kathryn: Hi, Nicole. Wanna sit with us?

Nicole: Are you sure?

Kathryn's Friend: Why wouldn't we be sure?

Nicole: Michelle and them wouldn't let me sit at their table ...

Kathryn's Other Friend: Their loss. Want a cookie?

**66** It seems like everybody would be happier if there weren't any cliques, so how can we stamp them out? **99**

Most cliques don't start with girls saying, "Why don't we get together and become a bunch of mean, exclusive, bossy chicks whom everybody envies and nobody can stand? How would that be?" It happens for a lot of reasons that we'll talk about in chapter 5. Those *reasons* are what we have to work on, and we will.

You don't have any control over the way other people act. I know, it's a bummer, huh? All you can do is keep your own power to be yourself. Most girls in cliques have lost that. You can pray for them, be decent to them, even love them way down in that fine place in yourself. But you probably won't change them.

The best thing you can do about cliques is refuse to be in one or be controlled by one. What if that leaves you without friends? Not to worry. We'll go there in chapter 4.

Remember that you don't have to deal with cliques all by yourself.

## YOU CAN DO IT

It's time to get your BFF or your CFFs together, or just make time to work on this yourself.

### What you'll need:

- ○ at least one copy of this book
- ○ lots of honesty (so you might want to pray ahead of time for that!)
- ○ your BBB (and if everybody is making one, you'll need your copies)

○ art supplies

○ snacks!

## What you're doing:

You're about to take a look at how cliques affect *your* friendships. You'll be adding to your BBB and making plans to stay out of clique-dom!

## How to make it happen:

Turn to "That Is SO Me" in this chapter and do the quiz together. If you're just becoming friends with the girls you invite over, do the quiz thinking about what you all *want* your friend group to be like. If your pals are not the type to sit around talking for more than about seven seconds, try acting out each item before you all decide on it.

Create a new section in your BBB called "Staying out of Clique-dom!" Use the map on page 54 as a starting point. Think about what qualities you would like to have in your friendship group, and write them at the end of the road as a goal to get to. For example, you might want your friends to be trustworthy, loyal, understanding, forgiving, and fun.

Then think about ways to achieve those friendship qualities, and write them along the roads that lead to those traits.

## CLIQUE-DOM

Talk about exactly how you're going to follow those paths. Who will you invite to sit with you at lunch? When will you not laugh at the expense of others? What things are you going to stop doing (eye-rolling, lip-curling, etc.)?

Pray together for God's help with that, because you're going to need it! (And if someone wants to write down that prayer, you can include it in your BBB.)

# That's What I'm Talkin' About

In your own quiet time, you might want to write or draw or even just doodle about what happens now with your friends. Here's some stuff to think about:

It totally feels like a sisterhood when _____

_____ .

We included a girl who didn't seem to have any friends when _____ .

We didn't include a girl because _____

_____ .

It feels like we're a little clique-ish when _____

_____ .

Now that I get cliques better, I think _____

_____ .

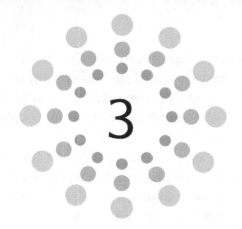

3

# Friendship Flubs

My mini-woman friend Rianna (not her real name, of course) wrote me this e-mail:

"I have these friends who I really love, but we are always fighting. Nothing serious, but it is really awkward when we don't know whether the other person is being real or sarcastic to cover how mad we are. Then I read Proverbs 22:24, 'Do not make friends with a hot-tempered person,' and I started to freak out. Does that mean I have to ditch all my friends?"

Yikes, no! If that were true, nobody would *have* any friends, because nobody is perfect all the time. In fact girlfriends, really close ones, can get to be like family, where you start treating each other like sisters. And if you *have* sisters, you know girl siblings can argue over stupid stuff and compete over even stupider things and totally forget that you're supposed to treat the people you love like, uh, you love them!

So, no, you don't have to dump your friends because you fight with them. This whole chapter is about the mistakes mini-women make with their friends—the friendship flubs—and how you can fix them.

## HERE'S THE DEAL WITH FRIENDSHIP FLUBS

66 Okay, so if I love my friends so much, how come I do such lame things? 99

# Who, ME?

Most of the time a girl commits a friendship flub for one of these reasons:

○ She feels like she's not important, and she wants to feel like she is.

○ She feels badly about herself, and she wants to feel better.

○ She's afraid she doesn't belong, and she SO wants to.

○ She's bored, and she wants to stir things up.

○ She doesn't always know how to treat people, but she wants to.

○ She doesn't quite know who she is yet, but she's trying to find out.

Check off the things on the list that kind of sound like YOU.

None of those are about someone just being a loser as a friend. Most mistakes real girlfriends make aren't on purpose. So let's look at six friendship flubs and see how you can fix them—instead of "ditching all your friends!"

66 No matter how large an argument or fight is, a true friend will always find out a way to break the ice. 99

## FRIENDSHIP FLUB #1: THE RUMOR TUMOR

## What it LOOKS like:

66 We had a walk-a-thon at the mall. It was pretty cool because we would pass by the same shops several times, and we passed by this hair place a lot, so we got to see this girl go from plain straight hair to beautiful cute little curls, and it looked adorable. So we were all yelling out random comments, "Nice hair!" "SO cute!" "That. Is. ADORABLE!" I observed that she looked younger, so I said, "It makes you look even

younger!" But the girls who were with me twisted it and changed it. THEY said they were whispering about her big fat, ya know, bottom, and all of a sudden (THEY said) I screamed out, "Yeah! Your butt makes you look YOUNGAWWWW!" (complete with the W instead of the R because I have a speech impediment). But it didn't really happen like that! So ever since then, whenever somebody is about to actually trust me and tell me some big dark secret of their life that they've never told anyone, Samantha will step up and say, "Julia can never keep a secret! You know what she did? We were at this mall walkathon, and ... (etc., etc.)" So nobody will ever trust me with anything, and I CAN keep a secret, ya know? It really gets to me."

## Just So You Know

Spreading rumors about someone is a form of bullying.

If you haven't been there, you probably know someone who has. It starts something like this:

- "I heard—from somebody who really knows— that she ..."

- "I don't know if this is true, but I kinda think it is: She ..."

- "Okay, A told me that B told her that she actually saw C …"

- "You are not going to believe what's going around about …"

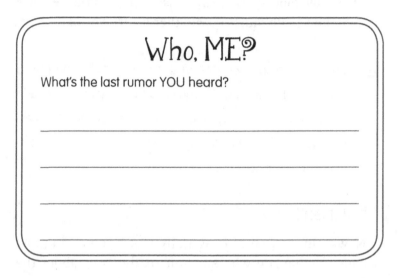

## Who, ME?

What's the last rumor YOU heard?

_____

_____

_____

_____

**What the Rumor Tumor is:**

As soon as those words are out of somebody's mouth, everyone else is leaning in—eyes wide, ears even wider—ready to hear the latest. This may be the second, third, or even fourth time the story's been told, but you can bet each time it's gotten a little bit juicier, just a tad longer, and probably a whole lot more false.

Did you know there's a difference between a **rumor** and **a piece of gossip**?

A **rumor** is a piece of information somebody passes on without knowing whether it's true or false. It could be something like, "I heard that if there's one more snow day, we have to make it up on a *Saturday.*" A rumor might be true, or a little bit true, or just a big fat lie.

**Gossip** is about somebody's personal life, and it's usually the kind of thing that makes people go, "No way! Really? Tell me some more." It's always passed behind the person's back and it's really hurtful, whether it's true or not.

> **"**One of my frenemies started this rumor that I had kissed this boy who had a girlfriend. This was in fifth grade, and why they were dating, I don't know! I had never kissed the guy or any guy for that matter. I went to the girl who started it and told her God doesn't like liars. **"**

## What it isn't:

News. Uh, *real* news is actually true—something told because the person who starts it really cares about the girl she's talking about. If the teller actually gave a rip about her, she'd be talking to the person herself, not everybody else on the planet.

## Just So You Know

The word *slander* is used when an adult purposely spreads a rumor about somebody to make that person look bad. It's like people running for office saying bad stuff about each other on the news. When they put it in writing, it's called *libel*. That might sound all legal and grown-up, but it's what tweens do when THEY tell lies about people.

## What happens because of it:

- ○ Lies get spread. Never a good thing.

- ○ The person being gossiped about gets her feelings hurt.

- ○ Some people believe the rumor is true, and the girl they talk about gets a reputation she doesn't deserve.

- ○ Once people have heard something from more than one person, it's hard to convince them it's not actual fact.

- ○ Girls have actually had to *change schools* because of rumors spread about them—by their own friends.

## Who, ME?

Check the rumor results on that list that you've seen happen or have experienced yourself.

## How to fix it:

It's actually pretty easy to follow these steps. As soon as you hear a piece of juicy gossip:

STEP ONE: **Find out if the "news" is true**. Go straight to the person being talked about and ask her. "People are saying you're being suspended for cheating, and just so you know, I don't believe it." Or just use common sense. Some things are so obviously false, they're ridiculous.

"Madison's mother has been married sixteen times?" Oh, come *on*!

STEP TWO: **If the answer is no, it isn't true, then simply STOP IT right there**. Don't breathe a word of it to anyone, and tell those gossipers they need to do the same. Start a new topic of conversation. ("Have you seen anything purple today?") Stand on your head if you need to, but do whatever it takes to snuff out that rumor. Most of the time all it takes is, "Everybody is saying Allison made all F's in the last school she went to. It just isn't true. Wouldn't it be awful for Allison if that got around?"

STEP THREE: If the rumor is true, ask yourself: Will it help the person being talked about if I tell this to someone else?

**If the answer is no, STOP IT right there**. So what if it's true? If it could hurt her or embarrass her, it is just *not* okay to spread it any further. Change the subject, and move on. Let's say Taylor has six toes on her left foot. You know it for a fact. But what good is it going to do Taylor for you to tell everybody? It would probably totally humiliate her, and there's sure to be some absurd boy-child who would call her a freak right in the cafeteria line. (What's up with boys anyway? That's a whole other book!)

**If the answer is yes, it would help her if you told someone, then tell the RIGHT PERSON**, usually an adult you can trust with the information. What if Ashley throws her lunch away every day because she says she's getting fat, and she's, like, skinny as a pencil? If she won't get help when you tell her she should, go to the counselor yourself, or tell your mom who can talk to her mom. You and your friends can't fix this for Ashley.

To make that easier to remember, here's a diagram for healing the Rumor Tumor:

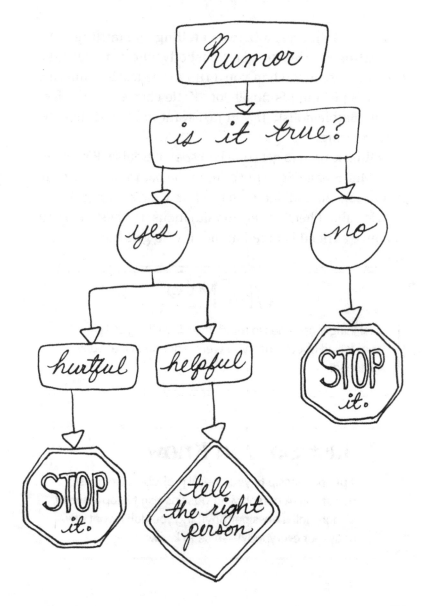

**66**If I tell an adult something about a girl, isn't that tattling? The teachers always say, 'I don't want to hear that'.**99**

There's a difference between **telling** and **tattling**.

**Tattling** is used to get somebody *into* trouble. Like back in preschool when you'd run to the teacher and say, "Joshie's picking his nose!" or "Katie chewed all the feet off the Barbie dolls!" If you just want to bust somebody, that's tattling.

**Telling** is used to get somebody *out* of trouble. For example, "Mrs. So-and-So, Amy cries in the bathroom every day before school, and she won't tell us what's wrong. We're worried about her." In serious situations, the best help you can give a friend is to tell an adult who gets kids.

# Who, ME?

First thing that comes to mind: the silliest thing YOU ever tattled about when you were a not-so-sweet baby girlfriend.

## Just So You Know

If people gossip **to** you, they'll probably also gossip **about** you. A person who gossips **can't** keep a secret, so don't tell a gossiper anything you don't want anybody—or everybody!—else to know.

**❝**Gossip is, like, all anybody talks about. How am I supposed to have any friends if I don't join in?**❞**

Sometimes girls forget that there are other topics of conversation! Trashing people behind their backs or even saying, "I'm only telling you this so you can pray for her," can get to be a habit. One that's hard to break.

So be the one to do it, but turn it into a fun game, not an opportunity for you to tell everybody how horrible they're being.

Make a list of non-gossip topics that you can throw in when the discussion turns to who did what to whom, complete with delicious details. These are some mini-women favorites I've collected for you:

- If you were about to have your last meal, what would be on the plate?

- If you could hang out for a day with any person in history, who would it be?

- If you were a car, what model would you be?

- What's the most embarrassing thing that ever happened to you? (And it goes no further than this group!)

- Have you ever ... pretended to be somebody else when you were bored ... fed food you hated to your dog or cat under the table ... danced in front of a mirror ... really, truly, totally surprised somebody?

- What's a toy you had to have when you were a kid and then hardly ever played with?

- What's a toy you just had to have when you were a kid and never got?

- What GOOD piece of news could you spread about somebody?

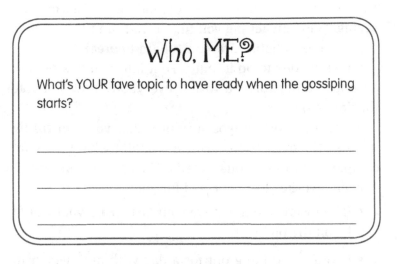

# Who, ME?

What's YOUR fave topic to have ready when the gossiping starts?

_____

_____

_____

Your rumor-spreading friends may look at you like you're nuts for a few seconds.

FRIEND: Did you hear about Emily? She got in SO much trouble—

YOU: Hey, if you were a car, what model would you be?

FRIEND: Huh?

YOU: Seriously. What model?

FRIEND: You're a freak.

YOU: I know. Isn't it great?

FRIEND: This is so weird. Okay, I'd be a Mustang. I think that would be cool.

But I guarantee they'll get into it. Aren't you into it yourself, right this very minute? The point of gossip is really to get attention because you have something interesting to say. So why not replace it with something interesting that doesn't hurt anybody?

## FRIENDSHIP FLUB #2: THE BOOTS AND THE DOORMAT

> My friend thinks she's the boss of everybody in the class. She talks to me in a stern voice, and when she wants everybody to wait for her to finish packing up, she says, 'Jenna, you have to wait for me,' like she is the teacher. But if I also take charge, she will get me in trouble.

### What it is:

One friend always gets her way. She's so … well, bossy, her pals won't argue with her. After a while, they just assume her way is the only way, which is fine with her. But, man, are they resentful.

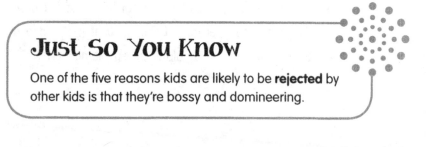

## Just So You Know

One of the five reasons kids are likely to be **rejected** by other kids is that they're bossy and domineering.

## What it LOOKS like:

It never ends up being pretty when one friend is like a pair of boots and the other one acts like the doormat she can stomp on.

> 66 Marcy and I were good friends, but we were so different and she got on my nerves a lot. I'm the friendly and sweet type of person, and she's the bossy and leader type of person. She'd always interrupt me in mid-sentence or put ideas in my head or boss me around, and it really got to me so that I forgot I was supposed to be friendly and sweet and just screamed at her. She moved away, and then I saw her at a camp. I should have been happy and surprised. I mean, what are the chances? She was actually excited to be with me there, but I did something totally just MEAN. I told her ... I didn't like her, and that I didn't want to hang with her. To her FACE. Not only that, but in front of her parents and her friends. Hello! Embarrassing! I want to apologize, but I'm just really nervous. I mean, what if she doesn't accept my apology? I wouldn't really blame her. 99

# Who, ME?

Got a bossy story?

_____

_____

_____

_____

## What it SOUNDS like:

Elizabeth: Hey, Sarah. You want to do something? Hang out?

Sarah: Yeah. Turn on the TV, and get us some chips.

Elizabeth: (to Sarah) Okay. (to herself) *Someday I'm gonna throw those chips in her FACE.*

**66** I guess I might be a bossy friend. I have this one BFF who never has opinions, so I always decide what to do. **99**

## What it isn't:

One friend just naturally being stronger than the other. Hello-o! Friendship is for equals. This is not mother and daughter or boss and employee or master and slave. We're talking friends here!

One friend making all the decisions because the other friend will never speak up. She probably never says what she wants because she's never *asked*. Or maybe she's tried and been told, "That's lame."

> 66 My one friend thinks she's in charge of our group just because she's the oldest. She needs prayer. 99

> 66 I have a friend who is the 'boss,' but she doesn't get everything her own way and when she doesn't, well, it's terrible. 99

## What happens because of it:

Both the boots and the doormat can wind up cranky after a while.

The Boots (the bossy one) ...

- ○ may get tired of making all the decisions without ever being challenged.

- ○ might get so sick of her friend acting "wimpy," she treats her even worse to get her to explode.

- ○ might be annoyed if Doormat does speak up for something she wants because the decisions have always been *her* job.

> 66 Nikki would always boss people around and get her way. She was tall for her age and smart and looked older than everybody else. Even though she wasn't exactly my best friend, I sorta felt bad for her

because everybody would always call her bossy and just sorta avoid her. She didn't deserve that. And, yet, I hated her bossiness! 🙶

The Doormat (the one getting bossed around) ...

○ will probably get crabby about never having what she wants, but she will more than likely keep that to herself ...

○ until she suddenly blows up and ticks Boots off ...

○ or goes off and finds other friends she'll probably do the same thing with.

🙶My friend Cassie bosses us around, like when we finish eating lunch, at least one of us has to escort her to the gym or she gets mad and throws a temper-fit. I know she does this because her parents just divorced and this is how she's dealing with it, but we're all 'bout fed up with her sass. Anybody have any advice for me? I'll take anything! 🙶

## How to fix it:

The only way for the boots and the doormat to stay friends is for both of them to learn a new word: *assertive*. That means saying what you want and what you need and what you think, but in a polite way, and avoiding statements like—

- "We're doing this my way or I'm going home."

- "You don't know. I do."

- "Do this … go there … say that."

- "Whatever you want to do is fine with me."

- "I don't care. You decide."

- "Okay. I'm stupid."

# Who, ME?

Give a real-life mini-woman example that could go next to the word *assertive* in the dictionary.

_____

_____

_____

# Just So You Know

If you're the bossy type, it will help you to use the *you* word more when you're with your friends.

"What do YOU think?"

"What do YOU want to do?"

"What snack do YOU want to have?"

## How to fix it list:

- Showing respect when your friend says what she thinks, even if you don't agree with her (in fact, *especially* if you don't agree with her).

- Listening to your friend, even if she goes on, and on, and on—and asking her to listen to you when it's your turn.

- Making decisions together instead of one of you *always* having to give in—use words like *negotiate, compromise,* and *cooperate.*

---

# Who, ME?

Write definitions for THESE words from the dictionary:

Negotiate _____

Compromise _____

Cooperate _____

---

❝All of the kids in my group have pretty strong opinions about things, so we don't let anyone boss us around. It's nice that way. I have to be careful not to be bossy because I have my ideas, but so does everyone else, and I have to also respect theirs.❞

## What an equal girlfriendship SOUNDS like:

Elizabeth: Hey, Sarah. You want to do something? Hang out?

Sarah: Sure. I'm thinking TV and some chips. What are you thinking?

Elizabeth: I'm thinking the chips sound good, but what if we watched a movie instead? I'm sort of sick of TV.

Sarah: Sweet. Whatcha got?

See the dif? Both friends keep the power to be themselves, but they don't *use* that power *over* each other. Yes! Sweet!

## Just So You Know

If you and your friend BOTH tend to be like "Boots," you can try using **decision breakers**.

- Draw straws
- Pick a number
- Toss a coin
- Play rock, paper, scissors

## What if you're the one in charge?

What happens if you're the leader in a project and you have to tell your friends what to do because it's your job? I don't think I can answer that question any better than this mini-woman does:

*"I often struggle with trying not to be too bossy. Several times in performances, I've been appointed dance captain.*

*That basically means I fill in when our teachers are gone and I write down the dances/formations. If any of the girls are having trouble or missed a rehearsal, I bring the group out into the hallway and review steps with them. It's a lot of fun, but I have to be careful not to be too strict with my classmates. Whenever I can, I try to make the girls laugh. Not only does it lighten the mood, but they're also more eager to learn when we're having fun."*

And then, of course, when rehearsal is over, it's back to everybody has a say and nobody is the boss. I like it, don't you?

**"** I may have come across as bossy before because I am a natural leader, and when we're working on a project and nobody's cooperating, I could maybe be, uh, well, be bossy. **"**

## Who, ME?

Who's the best kid leader YOU know? (Is it YOU?)

_____

## FRIENDSHIP FLUB #3: THE MIND-READING GAME

**"** I saw my friend at camp, and we were like great friends during the first day. And then all of a sudden,

she started treating me like dirt. She just avoided me.
I wanted to yell, WHAT DID I DO? Was it something I
said? Or does my breath just smell bad? To this day,
I have NO clue what I did. **99**

## What it is:

This is when friends expect each other to know what
they're thinking and feeling without having to say anything. It's like being best friends means you can see into
each other's brains. Really? Seriously?

## What it LOOKS like:

**66** My friend and I were at school, and it was lunchtime.
I didn't know what I said, but when we went back
to class, she started looking at me all oddly and not
talking to me. So I asked her what was wrong and
she says, 'Oh, you know what's wrong.' So I said,
'Actually I don't. Can you please tell me?' So she says,
'Oh, yes you do.' You get the picture .... it went on
and on and on. Then she started yelling. Well, then
I even had to write a letter to tell her I was totally
confused. It turned out she thought I had eaten her
cupcake, but I hadn't. We wasted, like, a whole afternoon over THAT! **99**

66 My friend came to my house for a sleepover. That night I think she said I could play on her DS. (I don't know if she did say that, or I just thought she said it.) The next morning she still didn't give me a turn, so I was all sulky, but I wouldn't tell her what was wrong because I felt sort of stupid about it. I was the please-read-my-mind girl. 99

# Who, ME?

Got a mini-woman mind-reading story?

_____

_____

_____

_____

_____

66 I'm not the greatest at understanding things like why my friends wouldn't sit by me at lunch or why they were giving me weird looks when I sat by another friend. I don't know why I'm not good at picking up these tell-tale signs. I suppose it's because I pay so much attention to who I'm with at the moment. 99

## What it isn't:

Sure, close friends can sometimes finish each other's sentences, but a true friend should be able to come right out and say she's mad or upset and why. Pretending to know what your friend is thinking is not a sign of being super close. Friends should not expect each other to know what the other is thinking.

If your friend can't read your mind, it's definitely not a reason to *not* be friends. Even people who have been *married* for twenty years don't know what their spouse is thinking all the time (and really, who would want to?).

## Just So You Know

Right now in your life, you're learning a thing called *empathy.*

You can sometimes feel what your friend is feeling.

You can "read" people and know what mood they're in or whether they want to talk to you.

You sense whether to make a joke or leave her alone.

But just because you have empathy, that doesn't mean you *always* know what's going on with your friend and the other way around. Talking it out is always your best solution.

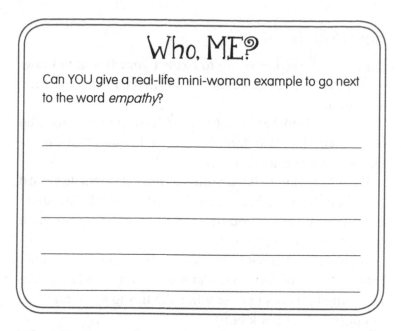

## Who, ME?

Can YOU give a real-life mini-woman example to go next to the word *empathy*?

_____

_____

_____

_____

_____

## What happens because of it:

Friends who fall into the mind-reading trap can make big holes in their friendships instead of talking things out. For example, one person might tell every other girl in the class what's bothering her about her friend instead of going to her BFF and working it out.

Eventually somebody might say, "Well, if you don't know, I'm sure not gonna tell you," and where does that get them?

> I sometimes have trouble with the whole mind-reading thing. I do NOT like fighting with my friends, so I'll keep things to myself so we don't have a big blowup. The problem is, that only makes it worse.

## How to fix it:

Decide you're not going to expect your friend to know what's bothering you. When was the last time *you* read *her* mind?

If your friend has upset you or hurt your feelings, be honest with her. You don't have to yell at her. Just calmly tell her how you feel and why.

Definitely don't share your complaint about her with everybody in your life. She's the only one who needs to hear about it, unless you first want to run it by your mom or another adult you trust.

If your friend expects you to read *her* mind, remind her that's not one of your many talents and assure her you're not going to freak out over what she has to say (and then, of course, *don't* freak out!).

Make a pledge to each other that you will always try to work things out.

# Who, ME?

Put a star next to the suggestion YOU really want to work on with YOUR BFF.

66 When I do finally tell my friends that they've hurt my feelings, they'll go, "Oh, I'm so sorry, Abby! We didn't notice we were leaving you out!" Maybe if I had said something sooner, I wouldn't feel bad for so long. 99

## What it SOUNDS like when you don't expect your friend to be a mind reader:

Nicole: Are you mad at me?

Hannah: Yeah, kinda.

Nicole: I wish you woulda said something. What's up?

Hannah: When you told Tracy I was spoiled because I'm an only child, it made it sound like I'm a brat. I'm SO not!

Nicole: Yikes, I'm sorry. I was just kidding.

Hannah: It hurt my feelings, though.

Nicole: I'll never do it again, I promise.

Hannah: Do you really think I'm spoiled?

Nicole: No-o! I was just showing off. Do you hate me?

Hannah: Hello-o! You're my best friend!

## FRIENDSHIP FLUB #4: THE DRAMA QUEEN

### What it is:

The whole drama queen thing happens when a girl turns just about everything into a reason to burst out crying or screaming or to declare all-out war. It doesn't even have to be over something big.

## Just So You Know

Tween girls aren't the only ones who can give Academy Award–winning performances when they get upset. Boys are just as likely to be dramatic, and since they bottle up their feelings longer, well, look out!

## What it LOOKS like:

"I had a friend who was, you could say, a drama queen. I met her at Family Camp for our church, and we quickly became friends. One day we were playing on a swing set. I was pushing her on the swing, and a certain way I pushed her made her fall off, which was entirely by accident. I tried to apologize, but she wouldn't listen. She stormed to her trailer and didn't want to talk to me. Finally, she let me say I was sorry, but she started hanging out with somebody else."

## Who, ME?

Draw YOURSELF as a drama queen (because we all have it in us!).

## What it SOUNDS like:

Susan: (in a low voice) Um, Cara, you have a little booger coming out of your nose. You might wanna wipe it off.

Cara: Thanks for embarrassing me! You always do that! Now everybody's gonna think I'm gross!

Jenny: Lauren took Ashley to the mall Saturday instead of me, and I'm her best friend. I'm not speaking to her until she says she's sorry.

Grace: Then neither are we. She needs to know what it feels like to be left out.

Lydia: We were both gonna wear our pink hats today. Where's yours?

Hillary: Aw, man! I forgot it.

Lydia: No you didn't! You left it home on purpose!

Hillary: I didn't! Honest!

Lydia: If you didn't want to wear it, you coulda just told me. Now I feel like a total geek!

## What it isn't:

Some girls just being more sensitive and emotional than other people. Okay, getting hurt feelings and crying over something important is "being sensitive." Having a total freak-out over every tiny thing? Not so much.

No big deal. During big dramatic scenes, hurtful things are said that can't be unsaid. It's like trying to un-ring a bell, you know?

Hormones out of control. Nah. Being a little weepier than usual could be from bouncing hormones, but we can't blame all full-out blowups on puberty.

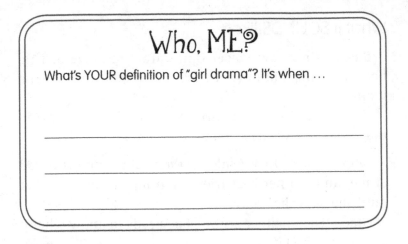

## Who, ME?

What's YOUR definition of "girl drama"? It's when ...

_____

_____

_____

## What happens because of it:

Other friends get pulled into it, and before you know it, the thing turns into a full-length, real-life play. Reality TV has nothing on the dramas girls can create!

Friendships stop being fun since there's always an issue being cried over. Those gatherings in the bathroom to talk your friend out of the crazy tree aren't really anybody's idea of a good time (except maybe hers).

Anger, fights, hysteria, and "breaking up/getting back together" get to be a habit. It's like you can't just hang out, giggle, or talk over actual problems because you're always in the middle of a soap opera.

Friendship makes life harder instead of easier. I'm not thinking that's the way it's supposed to be, are you?

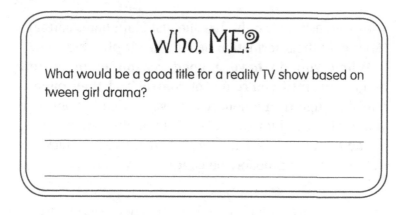

# Who, ME?

What would be a good title for a reality TV show based on tween girl drama?

_____

_____

❝ I usually am the one who blows everything up, makes everything go wrong, blames other people, and gets jealous of other people because they can have stuff I can't. I don't really like that about myself. ❞

## How to fix it:

If you're the queen of drama in your friendships, this might help you relinquish your crown:

**Decide what's really worth going off about**. Laugh off tiny comments that weren't really said to hurt you. Shrug away your friend's occasional bad day (because everybody has one now and then). Save your reactions for things that really matter, like somebody being mean on purpose.

Before you do react big-time to something (crying, gigantic sighing, saying, "Oh, no, you did not just SAY that!"), find out the facts. Does your friend know you're sensitive about that thing she just teased you about? Did she invite that other girl to go someplace instead of you because her mom told her to? Instead of just assuming she didn't sign up for softball because she doesn't want to be with you, ask if it's only that she just plain hates softball. Having all the information usually heads off a blowout.

**When you do have a good reason to be upset, don't wait until you're out of control and then pitch a honkin'-huge fit**. Be honest with your friend about why you're about to blow a gasket. Talk about how *you* feel, not about what *she's* done. By then, the urge to smack her in the face will probably be gone.

> I'm a drama queen a LOT of the time. I really need to work on it, but when I try, it just all builds up and then I blow.

Even better, try to avoid getting upset in the first place by letting your friends know what kinds of things you're sensitive about. "Could we not talk about me being chubby?" "Okay, enough with the teasing about my twenty-billion freckles." Just keep the list short, or your friends will have to keep a cheat sheet on them just to talk to you!

If everything really does seem to drive you nuts, or if you discover you really kind of *enjoy* tearful scenes and screaming fits, go to an adult you trust and talk about it. Sometimes the attention you get when everybody's gathered around you asking you what's wrong can feel good. Or maybe there's something going on at home that you can't talk about, so you let off the pressure by carrying on about everything else. Only a grown-up can really help you with that.

Remember that nobody's life is nonstop drama. A little bit of boring can be a relief!

## Who, ME?

Put your initials next to the suggestion on that list that YOU need to work on the most.

> I was trying to explain to my one friend why our other friend and I didn't tell her something, and she just turned around and ran off. My other friend started to go after her, but I held out my hand to block her and said she needed some time alone. That's what I would want.

If you have a friend who always seems to be in the middle of a soap opera:

**Let her know how you feel about her tragic performances at a time when she isn't putting one on**. Tell her you love her and want to keep being friends, but you're not in it for the theatrics.

**Don't let her draw you into a production you don't really want a part in**. Remove yourself from the situation or just say, "You know what? I think I'll stay out of this."

**Be really careful about teasing your friends, even though you're only doing it in fun**. That can set off not only a drama queen, but any girl who's sensitive about something. And really, who isn't?! Your friend may laugh a few times when you tell her she's a klutz, but a steady stream of that is bound to make her wonder if she really is and resent you for pointing it out. Teasing is supposed to be fun for everybody involved. If it isn't, find something else to laugh about.

## Who, ME?

Write one sentence YOU could say to help a drama queen in YOUR life.

_____

_____

_____

_____

_____

## What non-drama SOUNDS like:

Susan (in a low voice): Um, Cara, you have a little booger coming out of your nose. You might wanna wipe it off.

Cara: Yikes! (She goes at it with a Kleenex.) Is it gone?

Susan: You're good.

Cara: Thanks for saying something. All I needed to do was walk into class with that hanging out of my nostril. Benjamin Betts would call me Snot Nose until we go to college.

## FRIENDSHIP FLUB #5: THE GREEN-EYED MONSTER

**❝** I've been jealous SOOOO many times I can't say them all. **❞**

## What it is:

It's plain old jealousy, and it can show up with all its ugliness in a lot of different ways.

> I was always SUPER jealous of my friend Maggie. For one thing, she was super pretty. Everyone in the church knew her, and she was all popular. She would hang with the guys, and they would think she was all cool and tough. Then I would try to act all cool and tough like her and make a fool of myself. Then I'd try to be better than her because I was so jealous, and I would always end up failing.

> I had this one friend whose dad bought her EVERYTHING. She got the shoes I wanted and showed them off to me. She got a Wii. She got a rip-stick. She even got a motor scooter. It drove me absolutely insane.

> I have a really good adult friend who's like a second mom to me. I can talk to her about anything, and I know she loves me as much as I love her. One time I saw her with one of her nieces and realized they had a really good relationship too, so I started worrying that she loved her more than she loved me.

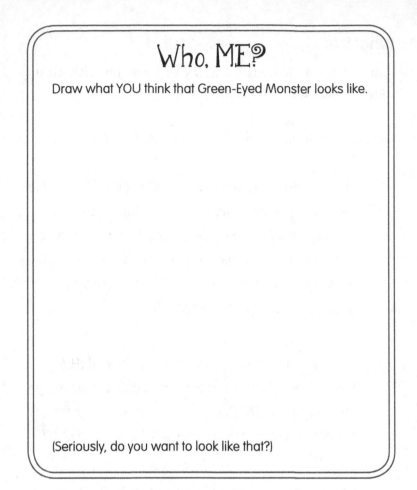

# Who, ME?

Draw what YOU think that Green-Eyed Monster looks like.

(Seriously, do you want to look like that?)

## What jealousy SOUNDS like:

Danielle: Aren't you just so glad Amber won the talent contest?

Jenna: I guess.

Danielle: I thought she was your best friend.

Jenna: She is, which is why I know her mom totally coached her and made her costume and everything. I could've won too if I had that much help.

## What it isn't:

> My friend at the dance studio is always saying stuff like, "You're such a better dancer than me, and I've been dancing twice as long as you have!" I try to tell her it comes with lots of hard work, but she doesn't stop. It's really awkward.

Jealousy isn't an okay thing just because it's human. Wanting to flush your little brother down the toilet is human too, but that doesn't mean you should go ahead and do it. No one is a horrible person for *feeling* jealous. It's what she does about it that makes the difference.

## What happens because of it:

The Jealous One may

- be resentful. And just like in the case of boots and doormats, that causes all kinds of problems you don't even know about until somebody explodes.

- feel guilty about wishing her best friend didn't have so many good things happening to her. When she feels bad about herself, it gets harder to feel good about anybody else.

- not be able to even congratulate her friend, which makes them both feel bad.

- talk trash about her friend to other people (which never turns out well).

> When my friend got all this stuff I wanted, I was so jealous that I started using her. I would try to buddy

up to her so she would take me places, like the movies and bowling. Most of the time, I just felt miserable, and I finally had to disconnect from her because of how I was when we were together. **99**

The Envied One may

- be hurt because her very best friend isn't happy for her.

- feel like she can't talk about her success to her friend, which is half the fun of having something good happen to her.

- try to back off on getting good grades or making more friends or whatever it is that's so great in her life, just so her friend won't feel bad.

- get sick of having to practically apologize for doing well and start avoiding her otherwise fabulous friend.

## Who, ME?

Which side of the jealousy thing are YOU usually on?

_____

_____

_____

## How to fix it:

> **Lots** of times when I'm jealous, I'm more than happy to go off and pout about it. It's like I enjoy feeling sorry for myself!

**Admit, at least to yourself, that you're jealous.** Instead of saying, "She just thinks she's all that," say to yourself, "I'm just jealous because I want what she has." That doesn't make you a horrible person. It just means you have something to work on (like every other person in the universe).

**Accept that everybody has both talents and flaws.** So why sit around wishing you were perfect like her—when she isn't?!

**Realize that jealousy, though human, doesn't make it okay for you to treat a friend badly.** It isn't her fault she's a whiz kid in math or the next Mia Hamm in soccer.

**Turn your jealousy into a compliment.** Tell her you're proud to be the BFF of the only straight-A student in the class, or the one with the longest hair, or whatever it is that you wish you could claim for yourself. It feels so much better to do that than to pout or put her down to the rest of the school.

If she's done something really big (like winning the county spelling bee), throw a celebration for her, even if it's just the two of you sharing a huge cookie and a card you've made.

**Develop your own fabulous talents,** not to compete with her, but to leave no room for wishing you were her. You'll be too happy just being you.

## Who, ME?

Put something GREEN next to the suggestion on the previous page YOU know you need to work on.

## Just So You Know

Jealous people are more lonely than people who trust their friends.

If none of these suggestions help, it would be a good idea for you to talk to a grown-up you trust about what's at the bottom of your jealousy. Most of the time it comes from not feeling very good about yourself, and an understanding adult can help you with that.

> A true friend doesn't cry herself to sleep if you make a new friend you have things in common with that you don't have in common with her.

If you're jealous because your friend has other friends besides you:

**Accept that it's okay to have more than one girlfriend**! In fact, it's a really good idea. No one person can be everything to you, just like you can't give your BFF all the things she needs from a friend.

**Know that just because she has another friend, that**

**doesn't mean she loves you less**. Does your mom love any of the kids in your family more than she does the others? Hello-o!

> A real friend is a person who sticks with you even if another friend comes along.

**You can make other friends too**. NOT to show her, that, fine, two can play at this game, but to make your life more full of very cool people. Is there somebody you can play video games with because your BFF isn't into them? Have you noticed a girl on your team who could help you with your passing because, quite frankly, your BFF has two left feet?

Be ready with a talk you can have with yourself when you find yourself getting all green about your friend having buddies that aren't you. "You're doing it again. Lighten up. She still loves you." "I love being friends with somebody other people like too." "I'm feeling all prickly, but I'll get over it."

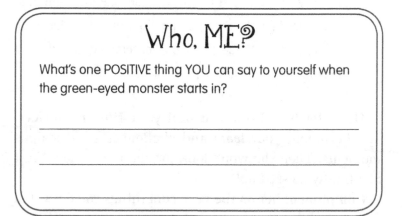

## Who, ME?

What's one POSITIVE thing YOU can say to yourself when the green-eyed monster starts in?

_____

_____

_____

> When I found out my friend has another really good girlfriend she met at camp, I started worrying if she likes her more than she likes me. Then I had a talk with myself and I said, 'Does me finding out about their relationship change my relationship with her?' And the answer was, 'Um, NO!' Nothing has changed in my friendship with her since I found out about THEIR friendship. She still loves me just as much as she did before. But I think if I'd made a big deal out of it, it would have come between us.

**It's okay to ask for reassurance every once in a while**. "We're still BFFs, right?" Just don't do it every ten minutes! (And be sure to tell her often how glad you are to be her gal pal.)

## If your friend is jealous of you:

> My friend says she's not popular like me and that she's really ugly and not pretty like me. I keep on telling her she's too hard on herself, but she doesn't believe me. Sometimes I get tired of it.

**Don't let her think you and your life are perfect**. Tell her about your fears and challenges—and jealous moments. Then she won't look for chances to say, "Yes! She finally messed up!"

**Compliment her on the very cool things *she* does**. Tell

her you think she rocks at drawing or can always give you the giggles.

**Don't say, "Oh, you're just jealous," when she acts all funky.** Sure, it's true, but saying that to her face will only make her feel worse. So will announcing it to your other friends. Try giving her some time. And lots of love.

Be careful about the friend who seems to think you are absolutely perfect, and thinks she isn't as good as you are. That might feel lovely for a while, but sooner or later she's bound to resent you because she's probably suffering from a low opinion of herself. Make sure she knows you aren't perfect and that you two are equals.

**If you make other friends in addition to her, let her know that doesn't mean you love her less.** Sometimes you have to be really specific and say things like, "Even though I hang out with Elizabeth on Sundays after church, I'm still spending Fridays with you, just like we always have."

> **66** I have this nice, talented friend I dance with. Well, she used to be my friend. She was always jealous of me because I'm really good at remembering the dances, so she'd go and talk badly about me behind my back. It's too bad stuff like this has to happen. **99**

If jealousy totally comes between you, tell your friend you'd love it if she didn't get mad about your being in the gifted and talented program or the fact that you have some other buddies. After all, you can say, you don't give her the silent treatment because she can talk to just about anybody and always gets elected class president. Ask if the two of you can just support each other.

# Who, ME?

One thing YOU could say to a jealous friend:

(Not "Get over it!")

_____

_____

_____

_____

_____

## What it SOUNDS like when you curb your jealousy:

Danielle: Aren't you just so glad Amber won the talent contest?

Jenna: Isn't that so cool?

Danielle: Is it hard, though, that your best friend got first and you got third?

Jenna: Are you kidding me? I'm making this gigantic congratulations banner for her after school. You wanna help?

# FRIENDSHIP FLUB #6: CLONING

> My best friend wants me to join chess club with her and not drama. I want to go into drama, but she really wants me in chess. I'm being pulled apart! Seriously—help!

## What it is:

The need to be totally alike in absolutely everything. Maybe one friend copies everything the other one does, right down to the snort when she laughs. Perhaps one friend gets mad when her BFF doesn't want to wear identical outfits, talk like they're sharing a brain, and be in all the same activities.

## What cloning LOOKS like:

> I've had some friends do that cloning thing. Ever since I can remember, they've been trying to be each other. Last year, we went to Disney World and they were planning how to be identical twins, like right in front of me. And you know what? They got really sick of each other and both tried, separately, to get me to be their twin. I was like, "No, I am an actual living thing with a mind of my own.

> My best friend ALWAYS wanted to copy me, which wasn't really a problem until recently because I seriously

messed up and did something bad, and she just copied what I did. She did it too and messed up her life as well. She has always thought of me as her older sister, and I should have been a better leader. I should have realized that my actions would affect her too. Now she's into all the other stuff she wouldn't have been in if I hadn't introduced it to her. I feel even worse now that I've stopped doing it and can see what it did to her. What have I DONE? ❞

## What cloning SOUNDS like:

Alissa: Don't forget soccer tryouts are this afternoon.

Jordan: I'm not trying out for soccer this year.

Alissa: Are you mad at me about something?

Jordan: No! I just really don't like soccer that much anymore. I'm taking some art classes after school.

Alissa: What am I supposed to do? It'll stink without you.

Jordan: We'll still be together all day at school.

Alissa: Best friends are supposed to do everything together. I hate this!

# Who, ME?

What's YOUR real-life mini-woman cloning story?

_____

_____

_____

## What it isn't:

What best friends owe each other. Yikes—even identical twins aren't alike in every single way!

> A true friend wouldn't tell you that she isn't your friend just because you like something she doesn't. If you liked all the same things, that would be so boring.

## What happens because of it:

The girl who wants to clone can get so clingy she becomes Velcro Friend, and that may frustrate her BFF to the point of screaming, "Get off me!"

One or both friends can cheat themselves out of expanding the friend group to include more very cool girls.

The one who buys into cloning may not try new things or make her own decisions, which means she misses out.

Friendships don't usually last when one girl hangs onto the other like a ball and chain, or neither of them can go to the pencil sharpener without her friend attached to her at the hip. Too much togetherness is going to suffocate somebody sooner or later.

## Who, ME?

The most annoying friend-copying EVER is when ...

_____

_____

## Just So You Know

Tweens and teens who hang out together a lot will automatically imitate each other. That's because even as babies, we learn to survive by imitating our parents. It also helps you blend in and be part of the pack, which goes all the way back to cavemen!

Naturally imitating and on-purpose copying, though, are two different things.

## How to fix it:

Show your friend that you admire her by complimenting her, rather than trying to be her mirror image.

Look at the reasons she likes you enough to be your BFF. Are you funny? Loyal? A good listener? Focus on those great qualities in yourself. What you each bring to the friendship makes it work.

> 66 I had a friend who was, like, perfect, and my friends often tried to copy her. I would think, 'I should be more like her,' and I started doing it too. 99

## Who, ME?

The most different thing between YOU and your best friend:

_____

_____

If you always feel afraid when your friend does something different than you, talk to an adult you trust. She may be able to help you respect and enjoy the differences instead of being frightened by them.

If you have a friend who wants to be your clone:

- Instead of asking her to knock it off, tell her what you admire about her.

- Without mentioning the copycat thing, have a talk about all the ways you two are different. Laugh about them. Tell her that you love what's not the same about her.

When you make plans that don't include her or make a different choice from hers, also set up a time for the two of you to get together later and share your experiences.

If she doesn't get it after some patient trying, tell her as lovingly as you can that your friendship can't work if she's going to keep stealing your identity. Hopefully, if you do all of the above, it won't come to that.

> **"** I love writing. My best friend doesn't. But when I won a writing contest, she was the one who jumped up and down with the same excitement and happiness I had. She doesn't understand why I love writing, but she gets how much it means to me. **"**

## Who, ME?

If you were going to celebrate the differences between YOU and your friend, what food would you have?

_____

_____

_____

## What being your own unique selves SOUNDS like:

Alissa: Don't forget soccer tryouts are this afternoon.

Jordan: I totally forgot to tell you. I'm not trying out for soccer this year.

Alissa: Are you serious?

Jordan: Yeah, I just really don't like soccer that much anymore, you know?

Alissa: I guess you never did love it the way I do.

Jordan: Anyway, I'm taking some art classes after school.

Alissa: That's awesome. Your drawing totally rocks. I'll miss you, though.

Jordan: We'll call each other when we get home.

Alissa: I can't wait to hear about it.

## FRIENDSHIP FLUB #7: WORTHLESS WORDS

"A true friend knows when teasing and bullying each other is different."

## What it is:

- Making promises you don't keep.

- Telling secrets you swore you wouldn't breathe a WORD of.

- Complaining to each other 24/7.

- Exaggerating the truth to make a better story.

- Saying things that are true but would have been better left unsaid.

- Teasing that hurts, even though you didn't mean for it to.

- Talking trash.

- Just plain old lying.

## Who, ME?

Number the kinds of worthless words YOU and your friends sometimes do, #1 being the one you do most and so on. Put an X on page 107 next to the ones you never do.

_____

_____

## What worthless words LOOK like:

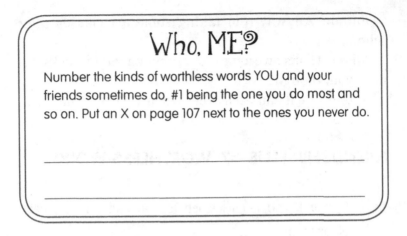

"A girl I know says that I am her best friend. I love her a ton, but what makes me angry is that she insults me all the time and then says, "Just kidding." I, unfortunately, use "just kidding" a lot too, so I know that you really mean the tiniest piece of what you say you're kidding about. It drives me crazy when she does that."

## Who, ME?

When was the last time "just kidding" showed up in a conversation with your friends?

_____

_____

# What happens because of worthless words:

- ○ A friend feels like she can't count on her BFF.

- ○ She stops sharing her private thoughts with her friend.

- ○ Both friends can get pretty crabby and see only the bad stuff that's going on around them and none of the good.

- ○ Both the lied-about and the lie-teller can forget what the truth really is and tell more and more whoppers.

- ○ The friend who just can't keep her mouth shut gets a reputation for being the Baroness of Blab.

- ○ The friendship basically stops being fun and safe.

## Who, ME?

Put a check next to the examples above that YOU have experience with.

❝A true friend won't joke about serious things in your life that you've vented to her in private.❞

## How to fix it:

It's not easy to stop tossing around worthless words, especially because it can seem like so much fun when you're doing it. Who doesn't enjoy coming out with a snarky comment like, "Hey, I found your nose. It was in my business"?

> Sometimes my friends and I throw words around like they mean nothing, and the next thing we know, someone's in BIG trouble.

Besides that, it's hard to stop when everybody else is doing it. All the time. Hopefully this will help:

**Make a pledge to each other to be careful with your words**. Be really detailed about things you need to call a halt to, like spending all your time together dissing other people or letting each other down with broken promises.

When the temptation arises to spill a secret or make a put-down (though hilarious!) remark, do whatever you have to do to zip your lips. Put your hand over your mouth. Leave the situation. Change the subject. (Remember that list you made earlier in the chapter?) Keep the duct tape handy. (Okay, maybe not that ...)

If you realize you just can't hold yourself back, let your friends know they can't share their secrets with you until you get a handle on your blabbing problem. Ask them please not to laugh when you make a funny remark that hurts somebody's feelings (even if it's some of your best stuff).

**Before you make a promise, really think about whether you can keep it**. Only say you'll do what you absolutely know you can deliver on. If promise-keeping is a challenge for you, ask your friends to call you on it when you cross your heart about something. "Are you really going to come through with that? Really?"

## Who, ME?

Draw a pair of lips next to the suggestion on page 110 that YOU need to work on most.

66A true friend will know when to stop teasing you.99

Basically, think about what you want people to say to and about you, and then say those things to and about your precious friends. Why would you want to do anything else?

## What it LOOKS like to make your words worth something:

66My best friend was really teasing me hard, saying things like, 'You are so retarded!' and 'Well, yeah, Genius. Du-uh!' When it wasn't funny anymore, I told her that, and she was like, 'Ohmygosh I'm so SORRY!' Now when she slips up, I just say 'NF' for 'not funny' and she goes, 'My bad.' I think she respects me more now too.99

66Jesus says, 'Do not swear at all,' which doesn't mean just 'don't cuss.' It means don't say, 'I promise' or 'I swear I will do whatever.' Just do it. So my friends and I are trying that. It's like we just do the right thing for each other instead of saying we're GOING to. It's working out. **99**

## Who, ME?

Name five worthless words YOU could erase from your vocabulary.

1. _____

2. _____

3. _____

4. _____

5. _____

## That Is SO Me

If you've been filling in Who, ME? boxes you're already thinking about your own friendships and the flubs that could be happening. But let's go in a little deeper to see what that really looks like.

# How's your friendship flubbiness?

This quiz is a little different but totally fun. Start at the beginning, and follow the flow of your answers. Don't forget to be honest, since pretending things are perfect isn't gonna help you much.

**Start [1]** Your friend is absent from school, and you know it's because of family problems. You ...

> **[1A]** don't tell anybody—even your cat. [Go to 2]
>
> **[1B]** tell the popular girls because it's the first time they've even looked at you. [Go to 3]

**[2 from response 1A]** Your BFF knows you know what's going on at your other friend's house and demands you share with her. You ...

> **[2A]** tell her you can't and switch the subject to her new kittens. [Go to 4]
>
> **[2B]** tell her the whole story so she won't get mad at you (because she won't tell anybody else, right?). [Go to 6]

**[3 from response 1B]** Your friend comes back to school and won't talk to you. You ...

> **[3A]** ask her what's wrong and admit what you did. [Go to 6]
>
> **[3B]** are pretty sure it is because you told her secret but pretend to be clueless. [Go to 5]

**[4 from response 2A]** Your BFF asks you to come over to see her kittens after school. You ...

> **[4A]** tell her you need to ask your mom. [Go to 8]
>
> **[4B]** promise to come even though you haven't asked your mom. [Go to 9]

**[5 from 3B]** Your friend tells your BFF, who tells you she's on *your* side. You ...

**[5A]** say there *are* no sides. [Go to 6]

**[5B]** tell your BFF the friend is too sensitive. [Go to 7]

**[6 from responses 5A, 3A, and 2B]** Your BFF tells you she's been invited to the friend's sleepover and asks if you were. You weren't. You ...

**[6A]** tell her you hope she has a complete blast. [Go to 8]

**[6B]** tell her you'll be SO mad if she goes. [Go to 7]

**[7 from responses 5B and 6B]** Your BFF says she wouldn't even think about doing anything with another friend if you don't. You ...

**[7A]** say you think you two should have other friends too, even though she's your BFF. [Go to 9]

**[7B]** agree that you'll never do anything without checking with each other first. [Go to 10]

**[8 from response 4A]** You are almost flub free! You and your friends have your issues, but you work them out. Keep it up. Your sisterhood is precious.

**[9 from responses 4B and 7A]** There are some friendship flubs you wouldn't make if your stuffed animal collection depended on it. But sometimes, just like any friend, you make some not-so-friendly choices. Ask your friends to help you be the best bud you can be, and do the same for them.

**[10 from response 7B]** As fabulous a person as you are, it's hard for you to avoid the friendship flubs. Don't cheat your friends out of a super sisterhood with you. Work on your "flubbiness" together. (Like, at the end of this chapter!) After all, you are great best-bud material.

# GOT GOD?

Even Paul, who, remember, was one of God's most trusted teachers, was concerned about girl friendships. Seriously. Check this out:

> I urge Euodia and Syntyche to iron out their differences and make up. God doesn't want his children holding grudges. And, oh, yes, Syzygus, since you're right there to work things out, do your best with them.
>
> Philippians 4:2–3 (The Message)

First, we have to get past the names. Who calls their kid Euodia and Syntyche and Syzygus? I'm liking "Nancy" more all the time!

Okay, now that we've gotten that out of the way, back to Paul. He goes on to say that all three women are excellent Christians who have worked hard to get the message of Jesus out. But they won't be able to keep doing that if they're all tangled up in girl politics. I know, even back then, huh?

Leave it to God to show them—and us—how to do the untangling. You've gotten a lot of suggestions in this chapter, but in case that's overwhelming right now (as in, you're drowning in it), Paul sums it up in this one "fashion" passage.

He says, "Dress in the wardrobe God picked out for you," which is:

○ COMPASSION

- thinking about your friends' feelings before you blurt things out

- laughing with them (not **at** them!) and crying with them because when they hurt, so do you

○ KINDNESS

- being nice to them even when you're having a really bad day
- bringing out the best in them instead of the worst, to make yourself feel better

○ HUMILITY

- not trying to be the boss of your friends
- treating your friends as equals because, uh, they are
- not bragging to them (although it's okay to brag **about** them!)

○ QUIET STRENGTH

- working things out without a bunch of drama
- not acting jealous when your friend has other friends besides you

○ DISCIPLINE

- not blabbing your friends' private stuff everywhere
- keeping your promises
- being careful about teasing
- not exaggerating, even when it makes a better story

○ BE EVEN-TEMPERED

- not turning everything into World War III
- being assertive but not bossy

○ CONTENT WITH SECOND PLACE

- celebrating when something cool happens to your friend

- refusing to compete with your friend (except in sports and games)

○ FORGIVE AS QUICKLY AND COMPLETELY AS THE MASTER FORGAVE YOU

- accepting that everybody has faults (even you!)

- talking problems through and then letting them go (No grudges allowed.)

○ AND REGARDLESS OF WHAT ELSE YOU PUT ON, WEAR LOVE

- loving your friend for real and never faking anything

Colossians 3:12–14 (The Message)

If you wear that God-wardrobe, mini-woman, friend-ship is really going to look good on you.

● ● ● ● ● ● ● ● ● ● ● ● ● ● ● ● ● ● ● ● ● ● ● ● ● ● ● ● ● ● ● ● ● ●

## YOU CAN DO IT

Bet you saw this coming: Get together with your friend or group so you can get to work on those friendship flubs.

## What you'll need:

○ this book

○ your BBB

○ art supplies

○ snacks

## What you're doing:

You'll be adding to your BBB (or whatever you're calling it) in a section called "Our Friendship Flubbiness," so start with creating a very cool page for that. Although it might be a little uncomfortable at first to admit that you're messing up some things, once you all get into it together, it's going to be all about making your friendship fabulous—and who doesn't want that?

## How to make it happen:

Decide which friendship flubs are the most challenging for the group:

○ The Rumor Tumor?

○ Boots and Doormat?

○ Mind-Reading Game?

○ Drama Queen?

○ Green-Eyed Monster?

○ Cloning?

○ Worthless Words?

Create a page for each one you're going to work on. On that page, write down your answers to these questions about that particular flub:

○ When was the last time it happened?

○ What exactly took place?

○ Why did it happen?

○ What was the worst thing about it?

That's the hard part. Here's the fun part. These are suggestions for each of the flubs, but of course feel free to use your own ideas instead (or also!).

## Rumor Tumor

Draw your own very cool version of the diagram on page 65.

(You can also make index-card-sized ones to carry in your backpacks.)

## Boots and Doormat

On a piece of paper, make a column for each CFF with her name at the top. In the column, list all of her best qualities, with a picture next to each one.

You'll get a visual of how everybody brings something to the friendship table.

## Mind-Reading Game

On a sheet of paper, make a column for each of these moods:

**Gloomy, Mad, Worried, Super-Excited, Upset**

Along the left side, list each friend's name.

In the squares that you form, write the things her body does when she feels that way.

You might have to do some demonstrating!

## Drama Queen

Make up a cast list for your friend group, like you see at the end of a movie, and give each girl a good role in the real-life story of your friendship (with nobody being the drama queen).

PEACEMAKER ... Jessie

LAUGH MAKER ... Amy

SHOULDER TO CRY ON ... Madison

(Get the idea?)

## Green-Eyed Monster

Ya just gotta draw or paint the best Green-Eyed Monster you can come up with, right?

Then make talk-bubbles over her head (like in the comics) filled with all the ridiculous things you think or say when you're jealous.

## Cloning

Take ten minutes to have each friend tear out pictures from magazines that just seem to be "her." Then each of you paste your own pictures onto a separate piece of paper in a collage. Check out how different you all are!

## Worthless Words

Put all the worthless words and phrases you have used (or heard people use) all over a piece of paper, as scattered and confused as you can. It speaks for itself, doesn't it?

**One more ...**

One more fun part. Come up with a special signal you will give each other the next time a friendship flub starts to happen. You could pull on your left earlobe if drama begins. Cough when an opportunity for gossip arises. Do a big stretch (arms over head) when jealousy starts to rear its ugly little head.

Decide on a reward you can give yourselves when you avoid that flub for a whole week. Could you pool your allowance and go for ice cream? Watch *Tangled* together for the forty-fifth time? Make it something you will all look forward to—and dive into it with all the fun you can have. You deserve it!

# That's What I'm Talkin' About

In the days ahead, write, draw, or doodle your responses to what happens with your friends.

We ALMOST flubbed (or did) when _____

_____

_____ .

The signal really worked when _____

_____

_____ .

Fixing our flub is harder (or easier) than I thought it would be

because _____

_____ .

_____ .

The flub I personally need to work on is _____

_____

_____ .

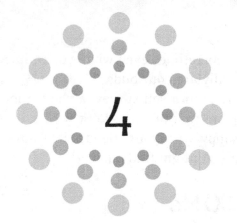

# Not a Friend in Sight

L.J., who is, naturally, a mini-woman like you, sent me this in an e-mail: "I changed schools this year. It was easier said than done, if you know what I mean. The first day was horrible, and I didn't know anyone. It was like that for the whole first quarter. Nobody really talked to me at lunch or during breaks. I walked everywhere by myself. It was like I was invisible just because I was new."

Whether you've been that "new girl" or had your BFF move away or just suddenly been left out, you're not alone if you've had that friendless feeling. It's worse than having a cavity filled or cleaning the toilets, right? This chapter is about those times when it seems like you're all by yourself, sometimes even when you're surrounded by girls who really are your buds.

Let's start with a self-survey, a chance for you to let go and explore that feeling. Work with it even if you're perfectly happy with your friends right now. You never know what you might find out.

# That Is SO Me

Read what's in each of the four boxes. Then put a big ol' star next to the one that best describes you MOST of the time. Don't forget that thing about being honest so you'll get the most help.

## Friendless in Girl World

Maybe you've just moved to a new school or a different class. Or your old friends have made new ones. Or you just haven't been able to find close buds to be with. Whatever the reason, you feel alone and empty and even scared. Maybe it's hard to go to school where all the "friend slots" have been filled and you don't seem to fit in anywhere.

## Friend-Challenged

You have friends, but you don't get along a lot of the time. Or maybe you don't like the way they treat you or each other or people outside the group. Could be you'd like to find other friends who are, well, nicer, or who are interested in having an actual happy friendship—but you haven't found any. In fact, you're not sure you even know where to start.

## Two or Three Is Company

You have one BFF, or maybe three of you girls hang out together. You're content with your little tribe, and you're not out there looking for new pals to add. Maybe sometimes you wonder what it would be like to have more girls in your circle of friends. Perhaps you even get lonely when your BFF isn't available. But most of the time, being two or three is just right.

## Miss Congeniality

You have a BFF, and a maybe a few other girls who are right up there with her, and then maybe you have a bunch of friends you love for a lot of different reasons. In fact, you can barely walk down the hall at school without saying hi to at least three people you could hang out with, no problem. Maybe it's a little crowded in your life sometimes, like when you can only have twelve girls for a sleepover and you can't decide which dozen of your close friends to invite. But mostly, you wouldn't trade your friend-filled life with anyone's.

**If you starred "Friendless in Girl World,"** don't give up hope. There are friends out there for everybody, and this chapter will help you discover them and show them that their lives will be so much fuller if they have you for a pal. Look forward to it!

**If you starred "Friend-Challenged,"** there's no reason to stay stuck with girls who don't make good friends. Friendship is *supposed* to be fun and happy and loving, not the biggest problem you have! This chapter can help you end unhappy relationships if you need to and lead you to the kind of friends you really want. Who knows, it could be with girls who are also "Friend-Challenged" or even "Friendless in Girl World." How cool is that?

**If you starred "Two or Three Is Company,"** get a big smile on your face because you are blessed. But don't miss out on the possibility of getting to know new people, including girls who are "Friendless" or "Friend-Challenged." They may not become new close friends, but you never know. This chapter will help you check out those opportunities and have even more good stuff to share with the sister friends you have now.

**If you starred "Miss Congeniality,"** keep reading. This chapter will help you be sure at least one of your many friends lets you be bummed when you're bummed and doesn't expect you to be the world's cheerleader 24/7. This chapter can also lead you in ways to make those who are "Friendless in Girl World" and currently "Friend-Challenged" feel less alone. If anyone can do it, you can.

## Just So You Know

People who know this stuff say that every kid will experience some kind of pain with friendships while they're growing up. It helps to know it's not just you, right?

# GOT GOD?

One thing is for sure: God wants us to have friends. God has provided people with good buds since the world began:

- Abraham and his nephew Lot

- Ruth and Naomi

- David and Jonathan

- Job and his buddies (Even though they didn't give Job such great advice, at least they were there for him.)

- Mary and Elizabeth

- Jesus' twelve disciples

- Paul's buddies, Peter, Silas, and Timothy, to name only a few

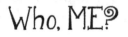

## Who, ME?

Which one of those Bible people would YOU want to be friends with?

_____

_____

The need for people to travel through a Christ-following life—or even just elementary or middle school!—hasn't changed since then. Jesus said,

> For where two or three gather in my name, there am I with them.
>
> Matthew 18:20

So, let's find out how to draw the best friends for you right into your life. As always, your fellow mini-women are here to show you that you're not the only one.

## HERE'S THE DEAL

> **“** We move a lot, but I never get used to having to start over every time. I just get all nervous and can hardly say anything. I'm just too shy. **”**

Not everybody is a total friend magnet, but these tips can help you when you're new or find yourself friend-challenged:

**Accept that it's normal to be nervous when you try to make new friends**. Even the girl who was voted most popular in her old school will wonder as she faces a class-room full of strangers, *Will they dis me? What if nobody likes me? What if I never make another friend my whole life?* Don't wait for those butterflies-on-steroids in your stomach to go away. Just take a deep breath, and go on to the next step.

Don't feel like you have to find a BFF the first day (or the day after your BFF leaves town or the minute your former CFFs decide you have the plague). Start slowly. Just as you're checking people out for possible friendships, they're looking for what you're all about too. The best things in life take time, including BFF-ships.

**Start by just smiling and saying hi to kids who seem friendly and girls you'd like to get to know**. Don't wait for them to come to you with, "Hi, wanna be best friends?" ('Cause that almost never happens!) You don't have to tackle them, either. Just let it show that you're open to meeting new people.

**Then start conversations**, even if you already know the girls around you and are kind of starting over.

- Ask the girl who sits behind you where she got such a cool backpack.

- Comment on the cute puppy picture the girl next to you has on her binder.

- Compliment that girl on the bus for sticking up for her little sister.

- Ask a girl you'd like to befriend to help you with something. People like to share what they're about with somebody who cares. It will give you a chance to get to know her in the process. A complete klutz in PE? Ask that girl who shoots baskets like she's in the WNBA if she'll work with you on your layups. Having trouble learning the names of the people in your class? See if that girl who obviously knows everybody will tutor you on who's who.

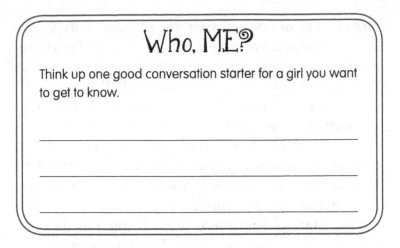

## Who, ME?

Think up one good conversation starter for a girl you want to get to know.

_____

_____

_____

**Listen more than you talk**. (You have two ears and only one mouth, so what does that tell you?) Ask questions and really pay attention to what that possible new friend says. If she sees that you're actually interested in what she thinks, she'll probably want to be your bud. Good listeners are hard to find!

**Be as close to the real you as you can be while you're doing all this**. If you pretend to be a certain way just to have someone to eat lunch with, you're in for friendship indigestion! Show the true you because people dig girls who are genuinely themselves.

## Who, ME?

Whether you're the new girl right now or not, name one girl YOU think is really herself all the time (or most of the time!).

_____

**❝** I hope you don't consider it mean of me to say, but I really don't think my best friend is that great right now. I kind of want to move on. **❞**

If you want new friends because your old ones aren't good for you, what do you do?

**Make sure it's time for a break-off and not just a case of a friendship flub that can actually be fixed.** You definitely need to part ways with a toxic friend—one who often leaves you feeling badly about yourself and bummed out about your friendship. But if there's still a lot of good in your relationship, see if the suggestions in chapter 3 can help you keep it together.

If you've tried to solve the problems and it isn't working, tell your friend or group good-bye without turning it into a drama queen scene. Something like this could work:

"Look, the way you treat me (or each other, or other people) just doesn't work for me. I've tried to talk to you about it, but nothing's changed, so I think we should take a break from each other. I don't hate you. I just think this is the right thing to do."

**Give yourself time and space to be sad.** No matter how bad things have gotten, at one time you had hopes for your friendships, and it's hard to watch them go away. Talk to your parents or some other adult you trust. Don't put down your ex-friends, especially to other girls. Just talk about how *you* feel.

Then make a fresh start by doing things like

- sitting in a different seat on the bus.

- asking your teacher if you can move to another desk (if you sit next to your former friend in class).

- joining other girls at lunch and talking about anything but your recent breakup.

- taking the steps for making new friends we just talked about above.

This time, don't settle for anything less than a friend who doesn't pull you down or hold you back; who loves you because you're you; and who helps you be your true, fabulous self, just as you do for her. No friend will be flawless, so just look for one (or more) whose flaws you can smile at.

# Who, ME?

Name one annoying thing about your BFF that you wouldn't change for ANYTHING!

_____

_____

_____

66 I had a friend who would sometimes leave me out of things and then at other times go sulk because I was talking to other friends. Or she'd read my diary or steal my lunch. I finally had to just stop being friends with her. 99

> **❝**I want to stop hanging out with a girl who isn't being a good friend to me, but when I tell her, she, like, begs me not to. I'm afraid if I keep giving in, she'll just keep doing the same things.**❞**

If you try to break off a practically poisonous friendship, don't be surprised if your ex-friend asks you to change your mind. If that happens, you might try this:

**Give her another chance if you think there's hope for working things out**, especially if you've never actually tried to fix the friendship flubs that have happened between you.

But ... stay true to what you know makes a good friendship.

**If you can't find a solution and you walk away,** she might turn on you because she's hurt, maybe by talking trash about you or trying to keep other girls from being your friend. Let that pass if you can and go on with your quest for better buds.

**If things really get out of hand, go to her and ask her nicely to stop.** As in, "Okay, here's the thing. You're only making things worse. Let's stop this before it gets ugly." Not: "Do you SEE why I don't want to be friends with you? Knock it off!"

If she doesn't stop harassing you, read in chapter 5 about how to handle girls who turn mean. Whatever you do, don't get pulled into her drama.

> All the girls I hang out with get along really well,
> except for this one who drives the rest of us INSANE!
> We don't want to hurt her feelings, but it just doesn't
> work when she's there.

A girl who does this kind of thing really can make you nuts. She …

- tries too hard to be funny (and almost never is).

- is a boy chaser (and can talk about nothing else, ever!).

- puts herself in charge (as in, she's the poster child for The Boots).

- just uses you and your group when she wants something (like an invitation to a sleepover or somebody to copy homework from).

- spreads the group's secrets to the entire school (and exaggerates more with every telling).

## Who, ME?

Think of ONE WORD to describe YOUR worst friend break-up ever.

_____

Do you do a group ditch? Not exactly, but here's what you *can* do:

**First make sure that what she does really brings the group down.** Don't make it about following "rules," like, "She can't buy her clothes at Wallmart and be with us." And don't let tiny annoying things (like her laugh that makes everybody in the cafeteria turn around and stare) overshadow all the great things about her. Anybody can be irritating if you spend enough time with them!

**If she really is making the group miserable, first try the appropriate fixes in chapter 3.** People can't change if they don't even know what they're doing wrong. Work with her, help her, and be honest with her.

**If that doesn't do it, the next time she starts in on one of her UN-friendly behaviors, be prepared for the naturally nicest person in your group to say something like**: "We've tried to tell you that when you do that, everybody's unhappy. So if we stop hanging out with you, it isn't because we don't like YOU. We're just tired of feeling funky." Then it's her choice. You don't have to say it, but basically if she chooses to keep on annoying people, she's going to be left out.

**Definitely don't be mean to her or dis her to other**

**people**. If she's hurting your circle of friends, distance yourselves from her in love and leave it at that.

**If she cleans up her act**, **welcome her back**. And resist the temptation to remind her of how heinous she used to be!

66 Three of us were friends, but one girl, Morgan, started talking about boys all the time and flirting with every guy she saw. My other friend and I didn't want to go there, so we told her and she got mad. We stopped hanging out with her. Now when I see her, she's wearing all this makeup and too-tight tank tops and hanging all over boys and she's twelve. I know she's hurting, but I can't be with her, you know? 99

66 I've been friends with the same people since second grade, and now that I'm in middle school, I want to keep the old ones AND make some new ones. I don't know how to do that without my besties thinking I don't want to be with them anymore. 99

It's really healthy to keep expanding your friendship circle. If you need a few suggestions:

**Make sure your present friends know you aren't ditching them**. Reassure them that wanting to get to know more people doesn't mean they aren't the best friends on the planet already.

**Don't force anything**. Look at the steps above for being the new girl and take them slow and easy.

**Think about things you'd like to do** that you haven't tried because your friends aren't interested. Then go for:

- that after-school activity that sounds interesting.

- those lessons your mom said you could sign up for.

- some fun thing your friends aren't into but that you're dying to try, like Rollerblading or sign language.

**Be on the lookout for girls who seem lonely.** You never know what you might have in common that could be the beginning of a surprising new friendship.

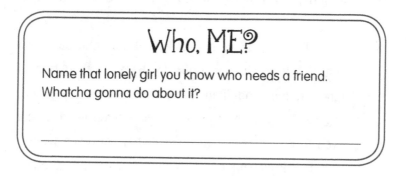

# Who, ME?

Name that lonely girl you know who needs a friend. Whatcha gonna do about it?

_____

66 Is it okay that I'm totally fine with the friends I have? (And I have tons!) 99

It's absolutely okay, but that doesn't mean you can't help make things "okay" for other girls. Maybe you could:

**Be the one who welcomes the new girl** and introduces her to everyone you know—since you know everybody!

**Ask the girl who doesn't seem to have good friends what she likes to do.** As the "social director," you can probably help her find someone to play chess with or who shares her love for *Lord of the Rings* or a could-be pal who also digs the trampoline.

**Encourage the girl who just split with a friend**. Be someone she can talk to when she's feeling low. Tell her what you like about her. You may not become her new BFF (you already have six!), but you can give her support in a time of change.

Make sure that while you're helping everyone else, you have someone you can whine to, cry with, and depend on for cheering up when *you* need it. Friendships—no matter how many you have—should always work both ways.

66 I was BFFs with these two girls, but then one day, they just decided I was no good to them, so they started ignoring me. And then it was like everybody except maybe five girls in my whole grade acted like I wasn't even there. So then I decided to try and earn friendship by displaying my gymnastics talents. I stood in the middle of recess and said, 'If you want, you can see me perform by the slide!' Nobody came except one girl, and then she ran back to her friends like I was a weirdo. No one my age is decent to me. 99

There's almost nothing more painful than being rejected, especially by someone you thought was going to be your friend literally forever. But it happens all the time—often like this:

- A BFF starts making excuses not to do things with you.

- She suddenly won't e-mail you back, and she's always "busy" when you call her.

- She or someone else tells you she doesn't want to be your friend anymore.

- She hangs out with another girl and acts like *she's* her best friend.

- She stops talking to you and ignores you, especially when the new friend is around.

It's even worse if her new friend is someone you've both been friends with and seems to have totally stolen your BFF from you. What's mega-worse is when a whole group of friends dumps you all at once. That's not just painful—it's agony.

All of the suggestions in this chapter for making new friends can work for you. But first, give yourself a chance to recover from an experience that makes you feel sick inside.

**Try talking to the friend who ditched you** (though you can just move on if you think that's best). Be calm and honest, and simply ask her what went wrong.

If there is actually something you've done that made her think you weren't a good friend, see if she's willing to work on it with you. If so, do the best you can to help your friendship without losing the real you. Chapter 3 can help.

**If there's no fixing it, walk away calmly without creating any drama**. Hold your tears, pillow-punching, and venting for when you get home with your mom, big sis, or some other understanding person (but probably not another girl your age). Take some alone time for that if it helps you.

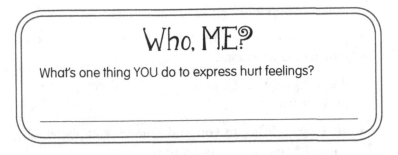

# Who, ME?

What's one thing YOU do to express hurt feelings?

_____

**Talk to God about it**, either with your voice or in a journal or a drawing. God can take all the venom you want to spew. Tell it all to God, just like the writers of the psalms did. Check out Psalm 109 for inspiration.

Then remind yourself that you are a God-made, God-loved person who is worthy of a friend who cherishes your friendship.

**Go back to your activities with your head held high** and, as you're ready, follow the steps we've talked about in this chapter for making new friends.

**Don't give up or avoid things you enjoy because your former friend is there**. It might hurt to see her with a new BFF, but you have a right to do the things you love. Your courage will attract new friends, and you'll feel better about you.

> **❝** I ALWAYS have trouble getting people to like me. I think I might just be an annoying person. **❞**

Okay, nobody is just "an annoying person." If a girl does things that make people back away from her, it could be because she ...

- is "different" from them in a way they don't understand. (Maybe she has ADHD or English isn't her first language or she has some physical challenges.)

- hasn't learned at home how to treat people. (She interrupts or pushes people out of the way because that's what happens at her house.)

- is having family problems that show up in the way she acts because she has no other way to get them out. (Her parents fight or she doesn't get enough attention or her siblings are mean to her.)

- is either less mature than the other kids (and can't keep up) or way *more* mature (and looks down on everybody else).

That doesn't make it okay for other girls to totally exclude her or make fun of her, as we'll see in our next chapter. But some of that can make it hard to invite her to the sleepovers and the birthday parties or to say, "Sit at our table!" when she constantly blurts out whatever's on her mind or grabs the food off your tray. And yet Jesus hung out with the people it was tough to hang out with.

So, a little help for you. If you really have trouble making friends and feel like nobody wants to be around you:

**Remember that God made you to be your own unique self**. Your job is to discover that real self and be her. In the meantime, God loves you as you are right now, this minute. And God will help you find that true you.

**If girls are downright mean to you, that's their issue, not yours**. Nobody deserves to be treated horribly. The next chapter on bullying will really help you with that.

But if you just can't seem to make and keep friends, and nobody is actually bullying you, it's time to do a little work to find that true you.

None of these are a matter of "That's just the way I am":

- Interrupting
- Always having to be the center of attention
- Criticizing everybody
- Using bad language
- Getting in people's personal space (like too close to their face)

- Blurting out everything that's in your head
- Being emotional about every little tiny thing
- Rude habits like nose-picking and open-mouth chewing
- Being way physical (poking, hitting, smacking, even in "fun")
- Always correcting people
- Trying to be funny
- Lying to fit in

So if any of those describe you, it would be a good idea to work on changing them. Get a grown-up to help you, because you probably do those things as a result of other stuff that's going on in your life.

# Who, ME?

This might be hard, but put a sad face next to any of the behaviors in the previous list that fit you.

(Then talk to someone about those.)

**Sometimes it's hard to make friends just because you don't seem to have anything in common with other girls.** Maybe you like to live in an old-fashioned world full of *Anne of Green Gables* and tea parties and costumes, and the other tweens you know are practicing to be cheerleaders and sending each other text messages. There is nothing wrong with either of those ways of being, but your way of being might not be as common. See if you can find out what *is* alike in you and them—you want good grades, you're Christians, you have a thing for cats—and talk to them about that instead of the things that make their eyes glaze over. Sure, they're missing out on a big part of you now, but once you get to be friends, they'll be more open to your special interests. And, BTW, don't turn your nose up at what *they* like. Be there at those cheerleader tryouts to give them support!

> ❝ I used to get so annoyed when people called me weird, but now I just take it as a compliment and say thank you. I would rather be weird than a person who just blends in and follows friends. It is SO much funner to be weird than just plain ol' normal, ya know? ❞

## Who, ME?

Name one thing you have in common with just about every girl your age that you know.

_____

_____

_____

## YOU CAN DO IT

Get your BFF or CFFs together or make time to enjoy this on your own. It's time to look at what's possible!

## What you'll need:

- ◯ your BBB
- ◯ photographs or drawings or pictures from magazines that remind you of ALL your friends—even those you don't see often. If you feel totally friendless, use pix of people you'd like to have as BFFs.
- ◯ glue or paste
- ◯ the usual art supplies

## What you're doing:

You're creating an "album" of your friends to include in a new section of the BBB called "Friends in Sight." You can do this even if you don't have close friends right now, but you have had in the past. If you've just never found good buds, create your gallery with people you would like to be friends with, even if at this point they're only in your imagination.

If you're doing this with your BFFs, you'll all see at the same time that it's not only okay, but it's good for people to have more friends than just each other. No single friend, or even one small circle of them, can be everything to you—just as you can't be everything everyone wants you to be.

## How to make it happen:

Paste the pictures onto the paper, putting as many on a page as you want, or creating a page for each friend. Leave space to write under each picture.

Draw or glue fun frames around each one.

Under each picture, write a caption that sums her up—like "Caroline, who always listens." Or you can find a Bible friend-verse that fits her to put there: "Brittany—A friend loves at all times." (Proverbs 17:17)

If you want to do more, do something to tell or show each of the friends in your album why she's important to you. Send e-mails. Make cards. Or just sit down and say it to her.

# That's What I'm Talkin' About

Write, draw, or doodle about what's happened since you added the photo album to your BBB.

I feel more (or less) _____

_____

_____ .

I've taken _____ steps to make new friends or to help other people find good buds.

I think I might like to make friends with _____

because she _____

_____

_____ .

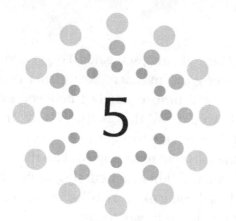

# 5

# RMGs (Really Mean Girls)

Mini-woman Hope shared this story with me and gave me permission to pass it on to you. You're about to see how brave she is.

"It started at my old school one day when this girl just looked at me and said, 'You know why I've never liked you, Hope?' and I was, like, 'Why?' (Stupidly.) And she was, like, 'Because you're so weird.'

"At first I just thought it was pointless. How was telling me I was weird going to change anything or suddenly make me un-weird, if you know what I mean? But then things would happen, like we were playing a board game called Game of Life, and I landed on that space that said, 'Get Married,' and she said, 'Forget about it, Hope. Nobody's ever going to marry *you.*' Other people started doing it too, and unfortunately I believed every one of them. Girls would say things like, 'Why are you even *here?*' and they'd make fun of the way I talked.

"From there it went to saying I did all these inappropriate things when I didn't and cussing at me. It got really bad, but I faked being okay. I smiled and acted like everything was fine when it was *so* not.

"When I stopped faking and my parents found out what was going on, they took me out of that school. But I couldn't stop thinking about their evil, malicious comments, and I couldn't stop hating myself because I felt so worthless."

Hope's story is only one of the many that I find in my e-mail inbox just about every week. She and so many other mini-women are suffering from one of the worst plagues in girlhood: girl bullying. You probably recognize it because you've seen it done, you've had it pulled on you, or, well, you've bullied someone yourself. This chapter is all about that. Let's start by taking a look at your own experience with Really Mean Girls (RMGs).

# That Is SO Me

As you read each behavior under "Have You Ever" on the left side, put a star in the column that's true for you. You might have more than one star in each row, and you may have none in some rows. Just like always, be completely honest.

# Have You Ever ...?

| | I've Done It Often | I've Had It Done to Me Often by Certain Girls | I've Seen It Done Often by Certain Girls |
|---|---|---|---|
| Decided who's in and who's out | | | |
| Suddenly excluded a girl from parties | | | |
| Suddenly excluded a girl from conversations | | | |
| Completely ignored a former friend as if she's invisible | | | |
| Spread rumors about a particular girl | | | |
| Gossiped about a girl at every opportunity | | | |
| Rolled eyes in disgust right at a girl | | | |
| Whispered about a girl in her presence so she'd know she was being talked about | | | |
| Pointed at a girl in a rude way | | | |
| Taunted a girl (not friendly teasing) | | | |
| Sneered at a girl | | | |
| Laughed rudely to a girl's face | | | |

# Have You Ever ...?

| | I've Done It Often | I've Had It Done to Me Often by Certain Girls | I've Seen It Done Often by Certain Girls |
|---|---|---|---|
| Threatened to exclude a girl if she wouldn't meet demands | | | |
| Threatened a girl with physical harm | | | |
| Deliberately accused a girl of something she didn't do | | | |
| Used phone calls or the Internet to intimidate a girl | | | |
| Asked other girls to shun someone | | | |
| Passed nasty notes about a girl | | | |
| Given a girl threatening looks or made threatening gestures at her | | | |
| Been nice to a girl in private but mean to her in public | | | |
| Ruined a girl's other friendships | | | |
| Hurt a girl physically on purpose | | | |
| Damaged a girl's belongings on purpose | | | |

# Have You Ever ...?

| | I've Done It Often | I've Had It Done to Me Often by Certain Girls | I've Seen It Done Often by Certain Girls |
|---|---|---|---|
| Laughed at inside jokes in front of a girl who wasn't in on them | | | |
| Given a girl an ugly code name | | | |
| Written ugly graffiti about a girl | | | |
| Acted nice to a girl to her face and destroyed her behind her back | | | |
| "Graded" girls on how cool they are (or aren't) | | | |
| **TOTALS:** | | | |

If you have any stars in the "I've Done It Often" column, you have been—and maybe still are—guilty of bullying. That doesn't mean you're a horrible person. It does mean you have to *stop* those kinds of behaviors and learn ways to feel good about your life that don't hurt other people. It can be hard to see what you're doing and even harder to stop, but you can do it. This chapter can help. There's a God-made, God-loved person in you who doesn't want to do this stuff.

If you have any stars at all in the "I've Had It Done to Me Often by Certain Girls" column, you have been the victim of bullying and maybe still are. It is NOT okay for people to treat you that way. You have done nothing to deserve it, no matter how many friendship flubs you may have committed. Hang in there, because this chapter will help you deal with bullies and feel like the strong, confident, lovable girl you truly are.

If you have any stars at all in the "I've Seen It Done Often by Certain Girls" column, you've witnessed bullying in action. No matter how you reacted to it, if you haven't done anything to stop it, this chapter is for you too. It will help you recognize Really Mean Girls and decide they can't be allowed to keep hurting people. Chapter 6 will give you ways to take action (that don't turn YOU into a bully).

## Just So You Know

One in every fifteen tweens has the "skills" to be a bully. Those are the same skills that could make them good leaders.

## HERE'S THE DEAL

See if you recognize this typical RMG, who takes part in any or all of these actions.

- ○ She knows what she's doing and does it on purpose; these are not accidental friendship flubs. This is deliberate, and it happens continually (not just once in a while).

- ○ She does things just to make other people feel less than she is; she has to be on top at all times.

- ○ She shows open dislike for people she thinks are beneath her (not as cool as she is, or as smart, or as well-dressed ... you get the idea).

- ○ She continues her bullying, creating a threat that doesn't go away and probably gets worse.

- ○ She can't stand people who are "different" (race, physical challenge, learning disability, or even just being from another part of the country).

- ○ She tries to get other people to shun her target, leaving the bullied girl isolated and alone.

- ○ She can act like she cares but only uses that to get what she wants.

- ○ She usually has a group of "friends" working with her (or *for* her).

- ○ She does her dirty work when adults aren't around; teachers often think she's perfectly lovely.

- ○ She refuses to accept responsibility when she hurts people; she never feels sorry and certainly never says she is.

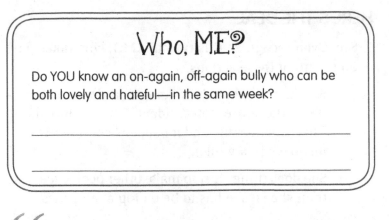

# Who, ME?

Do YOU know an on-again, off-again bully who can be both lovely and hateful—in the same week?

_____

_____

❝There's a bully at our Christian school (I know, right?), and you never know who she's going to go after next. What's that about?❞

Although anybody can qualify for this Bully Princess's cruel treatment, her usual target is a girl who ...

○ has some annoying behaviors (loud laugh, chews with her mouth open) OR

○ is new to the class or the school (which makes her "different") OR

○ is very sensitive (which means she'll give the bully exactly the emotional reaction she's looking for) OR

○ doesn't have a whole lot of self-confidence yet (so she's easily convinced she's everything the bully says she is) OR

○ stands out because of her race or religion or a physical challenge (which gives the bully plenty of good material for taunting and mean gossip) OR

◯ isn't easily intimidated because she's independent and speaks her mind (so the bully is challenged to take her down) OR

◯ is unique because she's smart, gifted, or talented (which means the bully has to make her look inferior so the bully can be the one at the top) OR

◯ just doesn't fit what the bully sees as normal. Maybe she plays with dolls; reads books constantly; has a big vocabulary; or doesn't care about clothes, boys, and gossip. This girl doesn't realize that, of course, the RMG thinks she can decide what everyone should do.

Um, doesn't that list cover just about everybody you *know*? In other words, if you aren't exactly like her, you're like a big ol' bull's-eye for this RMG.

## Who, ME?

Check off the things from above that describe girls you know.

That's a lot of checks, isn't it?

❝ The teachers and even my dad say there have always been bullies and we'll all grow out of it, but I just don't get that. ❞

The dangerous thing about RMGs is that they know they can create something like a hamster wheel for their targets, so their bullying can go on and on and the victim will feel worse and worse. It goes something like this:

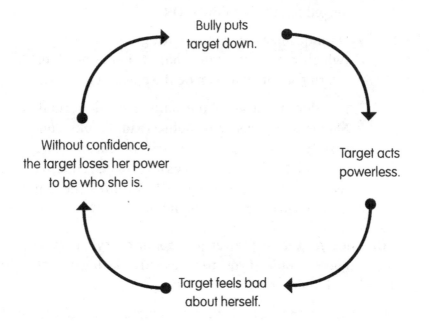

Bully puts target down.

Target acts powerless.

Target feels bad about herself.

Without confidence, the target loses her power to be who she is.

Each time this happens, the target loses more of her power to simply be who she truly is. That makes her easier and easier to bully until she feels hopeless. This is *not* just part of growing up. It should *never* happen. It causes feelings that don't just go away when the girl grows up. A girl who's bullied may do one or more of these things:

- She becomes convinced that she's everything the bully says she is; her personality actually changes as she believes she's a loser. How sad is that?

- She starts doing poorly in school or makes up excuses not to go.

- She becomes physically ill with headaches or stomach problems that can continue even when she's a grown-up.

- She tries to get back at the bullies and becomes one herself.

- She eventually thinks that nobody can be trusted (especially if the bully is a former friend) and from then on she has a hard time believing in real friendship.

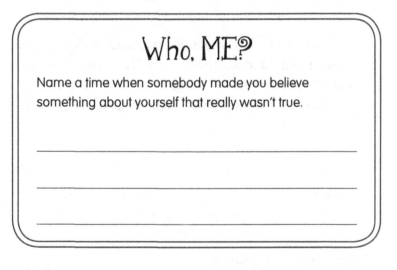

## Who, ME?

Name a time when somebody made you believe something about yourself that really wasn't true.

_____

_____

_____

I'm homeschooled, but I've heard about girls in public school that get, like, physically injured because of bullies. I'm supposed to go to public school next year for middle school, and I'm really scared.

That's bullying at its worst, and even though it doesn't always come to that with girls, these kinds of things can happen:

- Some girls feel so badly about themselves, they think they deserve to be hurt and they cut themselves on purpose.

- Violence—yes, actually beating people up—can break out in places like school buses, athletic fields, and girls' restrooms. The Internet shows videos of real girls fighting. How absolutely awful is that?

- Sometimes the bully starts it, but sometimes the girl being bullied gets fed up and starts punching. It happens in every kind of neighborhood and school.

- A number of girls in elementary and middle school have tried to take their own lives because they couldn't stand the bullying any longer and thought it would never end. Some of those girls succeeded.

> ❝I'm not bullied, but I know this girl who is, and I keep saying we should go to the principal, but she won't. I don't really understand why.❞

That's usually because:

- she doesn't realize it's bullying; she just thinks it's girl stuff she should be able to handle.

- she's ashamed that she's being bullied or that she can't do anything to stop it.

- she's afraid the bully will do something worse to get back at her for telling.

- she doesn't think anybody can really help.

- she doesn't think anybody *will* help because grown-ups really like this bully girl. (They've never seen her in action.)

- she doesn't want to be branded as a "tattletale."

# Who, ME?

Is there an unwritten "code" about "telling" among the kids you know?

_____

_____

_____

It doesn't have to be that way! You *can* stop bullying from happening to you. Let's start with how God can help.

. . . . . . . . . . . . . . . . . . . . . . . . . . . . . .

# GOT GOD?

Plain and simple: God is there to help the targets of bullying. He always has been.

In Psalm 55, the psalm writer has obviously been bullied:

> I shudder at the mean voice, quail before the evil eye,
> As they pile on the guilt, stockpile angry slander.
>
> Psalm 55:3 (The Message)

And not by random mean girls:

> This isn't the neighborhood bully mocking me—I could take that....
>
> It's *you*! We grew up together!
>
> *You*! My best friend!
>
> Psalm 55:12–13 (The Message)

Ouch! That *really* hurts. But the psalmist goes straight to God:

> I call to God;
>
> GOD will help me.
>
> At dusk, dawn, and noon I sigh deep sighs—he hears, he rescues.
>
> My life is well and whole, secure in the middle of danger
>
> Even while thousands are lined up against me.
>
> God hears it all, and ... puts them in their place.
>
> Psalm 55:16–19 (The Message)

He isn't finished venting. This is painful stuff that won't go away so easily:

> And this, my best friend, betrayed his [or her] best friends; his life betrayed his word.
>
> All my life I've been charmed by his speech, never dreaming he'd turn on me.

> His words, which were music to my ears, turned to
> daggers in my heart.
>
> Psalm 55:20–21 (The Message)

But things work out for him, and he has encouraging words for you:

> Pile your troubles on GOD's shoulders—he'll carry
> your load, he'll help you out....
>
> [God] I trust in you.
>
> Psalm 55:22–23 (The Message)

It's true. Even if you feel like you can't tell anybody else about the bullying, go to God and pour it all out.

Write to God in a journal.

Get it out in a poem to God.

Or just talk out loud into your pillow or at your favorite teddy bear. (Psalm 140 gives you a model for how to do that.)

Then be still. Calm yourself. You may not hear God's actual voice (that's very rare), but without even realizing it, you will be filled with God's love and protection. That will give you the strength to take your next steps to stop the bullying.

> All you need to remember is that God will never let
> you down; he'll never let you be pushed past your
> limit; he'll always be there to help you come through it.
>
> 1 Corinthians 10:13 (The Message)

● ● ● ● ● ● ● ● ● ● ● ● ● ● ● ● ● ● ● ● ● ● ● ● ● ● ● ● ● ●

# Who, ME?

What's a one-sentence prayer you could say when you see a bully in action?

Dear God,

_____

_____

_____

_____

_____

## HERE'S THE DEAL ABOUT BEING BULLIED

66 I was bullied a lot by a girl named Patty at my old school. She'd do things like write insults about me and pass them around for people to sign if they agreed. Then another day she would invite me to sit with her at lunch, and then halfway through she'd say, 'Why did I invite you? You're boring.' It didn't bother me that much because I had a best friend, Lily. But then all of a sudden, Lily was friends with Patty, which was bullying right there because Lily knew how bad Patty

treated me. Lily was trying to be friends with both of us, and she wrote me a note one day that said, 'I'm so glad you're my friend.' Patty saw it, and it was like the end of the world happened. Patty screamed at both of us and said she hated us and that we made her want to commit suicide. I know she's just saying that to be mean, but what was I supposed to DO with that whole thing? 99

Just a few more suggestions for handling bullies:

- Don't run away crying. That only gives the bully a reason to pick on you more.

- With your real friends, you can be honest about your feelings, talk things over, and work out your problems. *You cannot do that with a bully.* Bullying is about power. The *worst* thing you can do is tell or show her that she's hurting you.

- If a girl or her group shuts you out, walk away without making a scene. Do you really want to be friends with people who treat you that way? You *do* need to feel like you belong. You *don't* need to be with *them.*

- Don't avoid the bully unless you're in physical danger. Go where you always go. Sit where you usually sit. Do what you're in the habit of doing. Do not let her think she can cut you off from your own life.

- That may be hard, so ask some other girls to go with you, but don't become a bully gang of your own.

Everyone in the group should ignore the bully and focus on keeping you safe.

- Do *not* fight back. Don't try to give her what she's dishing out to you, because you're better than that. Don't try to show her who's boss. This is what is meant by "turn the other cheek."

> ❝ I had an RMG in my class. She was out to get me so she could have cooler friends, not messy little me. ❞

## What handling bullies LOOKS like:

Bully: Don't you have any mirrors in your house?

You (DON'T SAY): Yeah, want to borrow one so you can look at your ugly face?

You (DO SAY): I think you just feel like you need to be mean to somebody today, but I'm not your girl. (Then go on about your business, ignoring anything else she might want to add.)

Bully (to another girl, but loud enough to be heard by you): There's that little liar.

You (DON'T SAY): I know you're talking about me. Well, it takes one to know one!

You (DO SAY): I heard you, but I'm not listening (or just ignore her with a smile).

Bully: I don't know why you even come to school. Nobody likes you.

You (DON'T SAY): Why do you have to be so mean? I hate you! OR You could have fooled me. I have a lot of friends. OR Who peed in your breakfast cereal this morning? (As good as it might feel to come out with that!)

You (DO SAY): *You* obviously don't like me. Too bad we can't be friends, then.

Bully: No offense, but your breath, like, totally stinks. Ewww! Don't come in the lunchroom. You'll make everybody sick.

You (DON'T SAY): Oh, you noticed my camel breath? Nothing gets by you, does it?

You (DO SAY): I'm not going there with you. We're both better than that. (What is she going to say, "No, I am NOT better than that!"?)

Bully: If you ask her to sit at our table, you are out of the group.

You (DON'T SAY): Okay, okay—just please don't dump me.

You (DO SAY): Are you kidding me? You really think you can get to me with that?

What you're doing when you give those don't-fight-back answers is **taking back the power to be yourself**. You are a child of God, God's own kid. You're trying to be like Jesus, not like the bully.

## Who, ME?

What's the thing you like most about YOU? Imagine hanging onto that no matter what.

_____

_____

_____

**“**I don't think I can do that because some of the things this mean girl says to me are partly true. Like, I DO always have my hand up to answer questions in class and she's all 'Brainiac. You think you're so smart.' Stuff like that.**”**

If what a bully says about you has a little bit of truth in it, that *really* hurts. So … just remember that it's the *way* she says it that is mean and not okay.

When you're ready, you can consider whether you *could* be cleaner and neater when you come to school, or if you might actually stop trying so hard to be funny and just be yourself. But do those things because they will make you more genuine, not because you want to avoid being bullied.

If she taunts you about being smart or talented or mature, things you don't need to change about yourself, just know that she's probably threatened by you. You can walk away from that knowing it's about her, not about you.

## Just So You Know

If you're an always-has-her-hand-up kind of gal, you COULD look around first to see if somebody else wants a chance to answer the question or voice an opinion before you wave the teacher down. That's not changing who you are. That's just being considerate. Of course, if nobody else seems to have a clue, have at it!

> **"**I keep trying to be nice to this one girl who's really mean to me and some other people too, but she just keeps doing it. It's so frustrating.**"**

You're probably not going to change the bully. That isn't your mission right now. Your job is to …

- let God heal your heart, so you don't turn into her.

- be a strong example for other girls who are bullied (or are bullies themselves).

- become a person that no bully princess—or anyone else who pressures you—can dictate what you do or say or how you live.

> **"**Whenever I hear that verse about Jesus saying we have to love our enemies, I think about the mean girls at my school, and I think, "Sorry, Jesus, but I can't do that.**"**

Yeah, really. This RMG does all this dirty, rotten stuff to you, and you're supposed to love her? Could Jesus make it just a little bit harder, maybe? Before you decide you cannot possibly do that, Jesus isn't saying to go hang out with her, try to be her friend, let her stomp all over you. Here's what he's telling you to do:

Pray for her. Not "Father, please make her go cross-eyed and let a bushel of basketballs fall on her head." And not "God, thank you that I'm a better person than she is." Simply pray that God will heal whatever is making her be such an RMG, because nobody is born to bully.

Have compassion for her. That means feel bad for her

because she isn't seeing what a great person you are. It may seem like she has it all, including power, but deep inside she's really unhappy with herself. Being mean never gives a person joy, so she's actually pretty miserable. Be soft toward her in your heart, even though you can't trust her with your feelings.

Avoid telling everyone what a little brat she's being. She may be doing that to you, but as a Christ-follower, you don't get to do that to her.

Forgive her. Again, that doesn't mean tell her it's okay that she has made school a torture chamber for you. But don't hold hate for her inside you. That only makes you full of hate—hateful. Let go of thoughts of wanting to get back at her or needing to see her suffer. That stuff will go through your head, but allow it to pass right on out. Otherwise, she still has control over you. Forgiveness sets you free.

It won't be easy, but, then, nobody ever promised it would be.

## Who, ME?

List three good things about that RMG (even if it kills ya!)

_____

_____

_____

> **When I was a lot younger, I went crying to the teacher once and told her that the other kids were being mean and wouldn't play with me. And she said, 'Well, that means they don't want to play with you. Go do something else. Leave them alone.' She might as well have added, 'Doesn't surprise me. I wouldn't play with you either.' I've never forgotten that. Now when someone's mean to me, I feel like I can't go to anybody for help.**

There *is* help for bullying, and nobody should try to go it alone. Here are some suggestions:

If you don't have friends to stand up for you, you can enlist the aid of girls you don't know very well but who seem to be non-bulliers. For example, ask them if they'll just walk with you to your locker if that's where an RMG always waits to stuff your backpack in the trashcan. She won't do it in front of a crowd.

Find an understanding adult woman who can help you come up with a plan (based on the things in this chapter). There *are* some, especially if you say, "I'm not here to whine. I just want to fix this so I can get on with my life."

With her help, write down your plan and carry it with you. Because bullying isn't "normal," dealing with it doesn't come naturally either.

> **I get really scared when I think about girls who committed suicide because they were bullied so bad, and I wonder, *why does that happen*? Didn't anybody care?**

It's not that no one cares. It's that no one knows. That's why in certain bullying situations, it is VERY important that you tell an adult you trust what's going on and how it's affecting you. TELL if:

- you are in physical danger.

- the bullying is affecting your grades.

- you're physically sick because of the way the RMG is treating you.

- you feel so sad and hopeless you don't want to go to school or participate in the things you usually enjoy.

Remember that *telling is not tattling*. Keep telling adults until somebody helps you. Don't settle for "Oh, this is just the way girls are." Don't give up until some-one listens to you.

Don't worry that the bully is going to make it worse for you if you tell. Real help will protect you and everyone else she picks on.

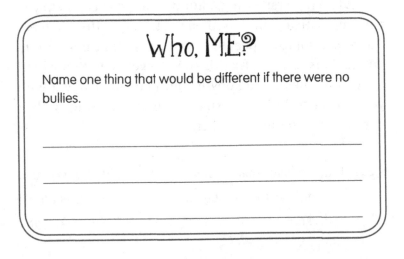

# Who, ME?

Name one thing that would be different if there were no bullies.

_____

_____

_____

# HERE'S THE DEAL ABOUT BULLIES IN CYBERSPACE

66 I don't have e-mail or a cell phone, but I've heard that girls say mean stuff about me on, like, Facebook (which they're not even supposed to be ON!) and in text messages. I feel left out, and I can't respond because I don't even know what it says. 99

**Cyber-bullying** is anything cruel or harmful that's sent by e-mail, Web site, blog, Facebook, text message, phone call, voice mail, YouTube, or online forum. It looks like this:

- A girl gets an e-mail—or even a ton of e-mails—putting her down or threatening her. She can't tell who's sending them.

- A girl receives texts from unknown senders full of bad language, insults, and statements meant to scare her.

- Somebody spreads a rumor about her on Facebook or even on a Web site. Hundreds, thousands, even millions of people can read it.

- Every time a girl turns on her computer or gets a voice mail on her phone, she's terrified she'll see another hideous picture of herself somebody has Photoshopped on the computer or a bunch of quotes from people saying gross, untrue things about her.

## Just So You Know

Seventy-two percent of kids eleven to nineteen report that they've been cyber-bullied.

All of the things that are true about in-person bullying apply to cyber-bullying, but in many ways, RMGs operating on a computer or cell phone have even *more* power to hurt.

- Instead of just the class or everybody in the cafeteria watching the bullying, everybody on the World Wide Web can see it!

- The girl being cyber-bullied often doesn't even know who's doing it.

- It can be extremely difficult to find out who the RMG is.

- The abuser might even be someone she least suspects, since you don't have to be big or the leader of a mean clique to cyber-bully. The bully can hide behind her computer and say whatever she wants.

- It happens right in the cyber-bullied girl's own home, maybe even her bedroom, her safe place. It can feel as if there's no getting away from it. She might wake up in the morning to a nasty text message.

- Being able to read and reread what someone has said can actually cut deeper than just hearing it once.

- It can happen without adults knowing what's going on.

- Other girls are willing to join in and gang up because no one knows who they are.

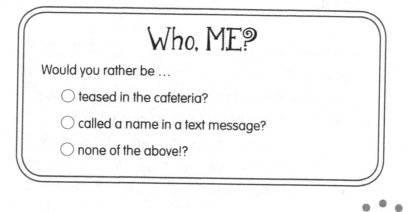

## Who, ME?

Would you rather be ...

○ teased in the cafeteria?

○ called a name in a text message?

○ none of the above!?

## Just So You Know

Symbols like these are used to make people feel bad in text messages and emails—and they aren't even words!

☹          ...          ;)

It's really sad, because the Internet gives everyone a chance to be heard, and some people have decided to use that chance to criticize or make fun of other people.

> I haven't even told my parents I'm being bullied online because I know they'll take the computer away from me. But I don't know how to make it stop.

You could just turn off your computer, but then you're cut out of getting information for schoolwork or communicating with your friends. It isn't fair for you to have to give up your e-mail because somebody's abusing it.

> One day I was playing a game on my iPod. It was like a chat room sort of thing, but these strangers started talking to me so I said, 'hello how r u,' like anyone should, but then they started swearing at me and telling me really nasty things, so I immediately reported it and deleted the game, but I was still scared to play on my iPod for like three days.

## Just So You Know

To stay safe overall on the Internet:

- Never give out personal information. (Not even on a safe blog like mine.)

- Don't give people you don't know your cell phone number, screen name, or e-mail address.

- Use a screen name that doesn't give out anything about your age, gender, or location.

- Don't exchange pictures or videos with people you meet online.

To AVOID being involved in bullying on the Internet:

- Don't share passwords, even with people you know. Others can use them, pretending to be you.

- If you see an e-mail in your inbox from someone who has bullied you, don't open it. Do save it (see below).

- Have someone show you how to block certain senders from your e-mail.

- Don't send a message of any kind when you're angry.

- Don't believe hateful posts about someone else. Just because it's on the Internet doesn't mean it's true. Pretend you never saw it.

If you're the victim of cyber-bullying, here's what you can do:

- Don't reply to any kind of communication that is abusive or obscene. The first time it happens, ignore it or log off.

- If it happens again, take action. Your service provider (that would be like Yahoo or Hotmail) should have a number that you can call to report abusive messaging. Have your mom or dad call it. You can even forward nasty e-mails to your service provider. (And yeah, at that point, you really do need to tell your parents.)

- If it doesn't stop, try to find out who's doing it. Using Outlook or Outlook Express, click the right mouse button over an e-mail to reveal details about who sent the e-mail and from where it was sent. Then get your parents to contact the school or service provider about the sender of the e-mail. Remember, this is telling, not tattling.

- If the situation becomes serious—you're afraid all the time, you're feeling bad about yourself, or you think somebody might actually carry out a threat—save and print everything that's said about you so that if your parents need to take action, they'll have evidence.

- If the cyber-bullying is happening on a Web site, find out who hosts the site and report it (with your parents' help).

- If the bullying includes physical threats, have your parents tell the police.

## Just So You Know

CYBER-BULLYING IS AGAINST THE LAW!

Depending on how the bullying is done, in some states it's considered to be harassment, stalking, and even abuse, which are crimes.

66 I got really upset when these girls had a whole blog about me that was really mean. But people, even some of my friends, were like, 'It's just a joke.' I didn't think it was funny at ALL. 99

Cyber-bullying isn't a joke. It's cowardly. People who do it hide in the Internet because they know what they're doing is wrong. Cyber bullies shrink like the cowards they are when they know someone is on to them. You are brave. You can snuff out their mean words.

# HERE'S THE DEAL IF YOU ARE A BULLY

66 After we talked about bullying on the blog, I figured out that my friends and I are kind of bullies, only we didn't really know it. We started out just being sarcastic with each other about certain people, and then it got to be where we were making fun of them to their faces and laughing when they didn't get it. Now I'm like really embarrassed about it. 99

If you have any stars in the first column of "That Is So Me" and you're reading this section, good for you! That means you're willing to face what you're doing and you want to change the behavior that may be tearing someone's heart to pieces.

What you'll learn here is not meant to make you feel like the worst person on earth. *What you're doing* is bad news, but you yourself are not necessarily "bad." You can change your behavior so that the true, amazing self you've been covering up can shine through.

You really have a responsibility to do this, because you can turn the power you've been using in the wrong way to something that can change the world for the better. You obviously know how to influence people, which is usually why girls sort of, well, LIKE to bully, SO why not influence other girls in good ways? In godly ways.

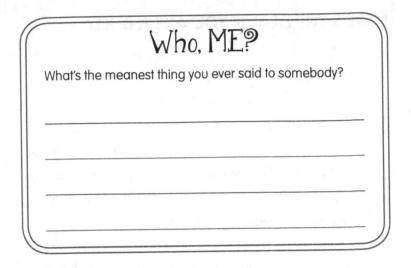

## What to do:

Accept the fact that you have no right to insult, intimidate, threaten, or abuse another human being. Period. No matter what your reasons are and no matter how much sense they make to you, it is *not* okay to bully.

Once you've done that, do not say to yourself, "I'm a bully." Say, "I've made a lot of mistakes, but I want to change."

Go to God, and pour it all out. Ask God to forgive you. Ask God to help you push RMG stuff from yourself so you can be filled with love and compassion and real joy. Do this every day.

Ask an adult you trust to help you figure out why you are mean to people. There could be a lot of reasons. Maybe you're bullied at home. Or your mom and dad let you pretty much run over them. Or you were bullied at your last school, and you aren't going to let it happen again. Could be you're so afraid people are going to find out something weak in you, you try to show them how powerful you are. You might even think people in general are out to hurt you, so you might as well hurt them first. Whatever your reasons, you probably won't be able to sort them out yourself. Please find a grown-up who will help you, not just tell you you'd better shape up.

While you're working on yourself with a helper, do these things as you're strong enough:

○ Go to the girls you've hurt and ask for their forgiveness. Don't expect them all to hug you and say, "Oh, it's okay." What matters is that you do it. It will soften you inside.

○ Tell your bully-mates that you aren't going to be mean to other girls any more. If that means they don't want to be your friends, that's okay. They weren't your true buds to begin with. You might be alone for a while, but as people see that you're really working on your meanness issues, you'll be surprised who will want to be around you. After all, you have a lot of personal power, and people like that when it's used the Jesus way.

○ Get rid of anything in your life that triggers mean behavior on your part. If you swear, make a vow to stop cussing. If you get mad when you play sports, back off on playing until you have more control. If certain people just bring out the worst in you, avoid them. It's hard, but it's going to be worth it when you can do all the things you enjoy and let other people enjoy them too.

○ Keep a mirror in your pocket or backpack. Every time you feel that strong urge to tell someone just exactly what you think is wrong with her, pull out your mirror and sneer into it. Do you really want to look that way? Really?

## Just So You Know

It's actually possible to be a Christian bully by looking down on girls who don't know Christ, excluding them from your circle of church friends, telling them God doesn't love them, or gossiping that they're atheists. Pray for girls who haven't gotten to know God yet. Be willing to talk to them about how great God is if they want to hear. Even invite them to church. But if you act as if they are poison ivy, that's bullying. Stop.

## YOU CAN DO IT

It's time to figure out if you and your BFFs are, as a group, bullies, bullied, or bystanders. Get the crew together!

## What you'll need:

○ this book

○ your BBB

○ art supplies

## What you're doing:

This is a new section in your BBB called "Bullies, Bullied, or Bystanders?" (so start by creating that cover page, maybe with some pix from magazines). You're going to find out that:

○ Maybe what you do on your own is different from what you do as a group, which can be either a good thing or a not-so-good thing.

○ You're not alone as you try to make changes.

○ Once you start being honest with each other, being your best selves becomes easier, and being your not-so-best selves gets harder!

## How to make it happen:

Do the "That Is SO Me" survey on pages 150–154 as a pair or a group. (If you're doing this on your own, just refer to your answers.) Try to come to an agreement on each item. Your answers may be different from what you starred on your own.

Look at your score and create a page from the list below for your BBB that matches that score. Of course, you can do all three if you want.

### Bystanders

As a group, you see bullying happening to other people, but you haven't done anything to stop it.

Write down the names of the RMGs you've observed. (Don't gossip about them while you're doing this!) Under each name, list her good qualities. Add anything you know that might be causing her to be a bully.

Do the same for girls you've seen who are bullied.

Add pictures if you want.

## Bullies

As a group, you discover you are bullies.

Using the steps in this chapter under "Here's the Deal If You Are a Bully," write out a five-step plan for shaking the bully habit. Make the steps things you can actually check off as you complete them (not just "don't bully anymore").

## Bullied

As a group, you find that you are the bullied.

Using the steps in this chapter under "Here's the Deal About Being Bullied," write out a five-step plan for becoming bully-free.

Make the steps things you can actually check off as you complete them (not just "don't let it bother us anymore").

No matter what category you fall into, as a pair or group or on your own, ask an adult you all trust to be your mentor in this. She won't take the steps for you, but she'll be there to support you and keep you going. After all, she's probably been where you are.

# That's What I'm Talkin' About

Write, draw, or doodle about what happens after you start on your plan.

I feel a lot more (or less) _____

_____ .

One thing that has changed is _____

_____ .

We have gotten help from _____

_____ .

# There Are No Innocent Bystanders!

Will you read this post from your fellow mini-woman very carefully?

"I have hated myself so much that I cut myself and attempted suicide three times—all from bullying. So many people just stand around and do nothing about it, but their ignorance and just watching it happen can cost a life. I'm better now. God is helping me. But sometimes I still just get super sad and start hating myself again and believing those bullies' lies. I wish that when I was bullied, somebody could have helped me. That's why I try to help anybody else who is bullied."

A famous man named Abraham Heschel once said, "Few are guilty, but all are responsible." Even if you're not a bully yourself and wouldn't dream of being mean to anyone, you still have a job to do. You need to stand up for those who are being bullied and do whatever you can to make your community a safe place, where nobody has to hate herself because of the way she's treated.

This chapter is about how you can do that.

> **"**Christians are supposed to be LIGHT. We are supposed to shine Jesus. But so many times we are just so caught up in our own little world that we fail to see other people's problems and confusion. And sometimes they can be pretty serious.**"**

## GOT GOD?

God is very clear that you need to take action when a girl is being mistreated by RMGs:

> This is war, and there is no neutral ground.... If you're not helping, you're making things worse.
>
> Matthew 12:30 (The Message)

Wait! Don't gather every girl you know and arm yourselves to go after the RMGs! Jesus isn't saying you should declare war on the bullies. He's telling you to fight against bullying itself.

> Don't let evil get the best of you; get the best of evil by doing good.
>
> Romans 12:21 (The Message)

Get the best of evil, not the evil *person*. And make that happen by *doing good*.

Before you read on to find out what that can look like in your situation, be sure your mind is ready.

> Whatever is true, whatever is noble, whatever is right, whatever is pure, whatever is lovely, whatever is admirable—if anything is excellent or praiseworthy— think about such things.... Put [them] into practice. And the God of peace will be with you.
>
> Philippians 4:8–9

That gives new meaning to the word *whatever*, doesn't it? Fill your head, your heart, yourself with good stuff— God stuff—and you won't go charging in like, well, like a bully. Helping girls who are being bullied is all about taking away the *power* of bullying. That's true and noble and right and pure and admirable. It's excellent, and God will help you. If you fill yourself with thoughts of getting revenge, seeing RMGs go down, and taking over their turf, don't count on God to back you up.

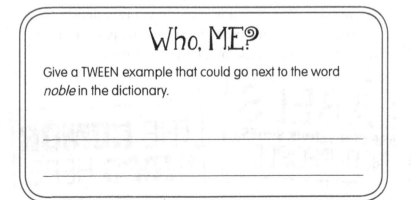

## Who, ME?

Give a TWEEN example that could go next to the word *noble* in the dictionary.

_____

_____

## HERE'S THE DEAL FOR STANDING UP AGAINST BULLYING

There have always been RMGs and peer abuse, but that doesn't mean it's okay. There used to be slavery in the US, but somebody put a stop to that, right? Yours can be the generation that stops *this* cruel behavior, so that you and the girls who come after you can grow up without being scarred by your own kind.

### Just So You Know

Bullying is at its worst in sixth and seventh grades.

But its effects go on for years after.

Here are some simple steps to help stop bullying. They aren't always easy, but you don't have to be a rocket scientist to follow them.

STEP ONE: Refuse to participate in any kind of bullying yourself. You probably wouldn't intentionally try to hurt someone, but it's possible to become part of the very thing you're against. So make these your slogans:

**YOU HAVE ENTERED A NO PUT-DOWN JOKES ZONE.**

**This is a school, NOT A BATTLEGROUND.**

**JESUS IS OUR LEADER**

## Who, ME?

Your own anti-bullying slogan goes here:

_____

_____

_____

_____

STEP TWO: Tell other people that bullying is wrong— in a way loud voice if you have to. Don't attack the *bully*, just the *bullying*.

> *I go to a small Christian school where we've all known each other our whole lives. One time I got so sick of the girls being mean to each other that I just stood up on the bleachers during PE and said, 'We're all we've got! We have to stop this!' And some of them did, at least so far.*

STEP THREE: Ask other people to stop standing by and doing nothing when they see bullying. Since fifteen percent of the girls do the bullying, and ten percent are being bullied, that leaves seventy-five percent of you "in the middle." That's a lot of bully-stopping power!

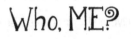

## Who, ME?

Count the number of girls in your class or church or sports team who are "in the middle."

_____

_____

STEP FOUR: Include people who seem friendless. They are prime targets for bullies, and you can stop it before it starts by helping an isolated girl build her confidence. Make it your mission never to let anyone feel left out. That kind of generous living spreads, and other girls will start doing it too. Keep thinking about what Jesus said:

> Whenever you did one of these things to someone overlooked or ignored, that was me—you did it to me.
>
> Matthew 25:40 (The Message)

Remember that if a girl ignores her bully, the bully will find someone else to be mean to. Your attitude about bullying can give the bully no place to go where her bad treatment will be tolerated.

## Just So You Know

Studies show that the whole school's academic performance goes up when bullying isn't a threat.

STEP FIVE: Get yourself an anti-bullying buddy (or group), and decide that as a team you will take action when you see bullying. You have numbers on your side, so get organized!

> " I have helped some people who have been bullied by being their friend and allowing them to just vent to me about anything, because sometimes we girls just need to VENT to someone. "

## Ways to take action:

Apologize to the girl who's been harmed in the past if you were there and you did nothing to stop it. Assure her that you won't let the bullying continue.

Rather than get all feisty for a fight, be as genuinely

nice, friendly, and inclusive to the girl as you can, even if she does annoying things or you and your friends have nothing in common with her. You don't have to be her BFF. Just let her know she's safe from ugly talk and physical harm when she's with you. Sometimes the bullying will stop once the RMG sees that her target has friends.

If your bullied friend is afraid to go someplace in school because she knows the RMGs will abuse her with their words and mean looks, go with her as a group. Surround her with laughter and happy chatter. No need to make a verbal statement to the RMG like, "Just so you know, your bullying days are over." Shield the bullied girl with your love. That's all.

If the bully does her thing right there in front of you, *then* stand up to her. Be calm. Be polite. Look her straight in the eye, but don't do anything threatening. Simply say, "Look, this is wrong, and we're not going to stand by and let you control people anymore."

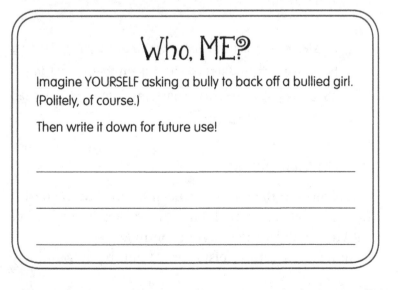

## Who, ME?

Imagine YOURSELF asking a bully to back off a bullied girl. (Politely, of course.)

Then write it down for future use!

_____

_____

_____

## How to help the bullied girl stand up for herself next time:

Take her through chapter 5. Do role-plays with her so she feels what it's like to be assertive. (Remember that word?) If she knows you have her back, she'll have more confidence. Love does that for people.

Encourage her to talk to an adult at the place where it's happening (school, church, sports team, etc.). It's important to make the grown-ups in charge aware of what's going on, even if you don't want them to intervene yet.

If things turn really ugly—somebody starts hitting or a mob forms—get an adult *immediately*. It doesn't matter if it's the maintenance guy, some mom passing through, or the principal's secretary, get the nearest grown-up. Physical violence is not something kids should try to handle on their own.

> The teachers at my school just write people up when they get caught bullying, but they don't really do anything to keep it from happening. It's like always the same people too.

That's a tough one, but there are things you can do:

• Show the adults this book.

• Tell them that you want to stamp out bullying totally, not just get a particular bully in trouble.

• Ask them if they want a bully-free environment for kids. I guarantee you they won't say no!

**66** I saw a lot of bullying going on in my old school. Like, even teachers would look down on that one not-so-pretty girl and would treat the other 'drop-dead gorgeous' one like an angel. **99**

# Who, ME?

Name an adult YOU think would be proud to help you with anti-bullying.

_____

_____

_____

_____

_____

**66** I'm still afraid that if I stick up for a girl who's being bullied, I'll be the next one they pick on. I've seen them turn on people so fast. **99**

Here's the thing: If you have other girls working with you against bullying in *general*, not specific girls (and especially if you've involved adults), there's no need to be afraid you'll be the bully's next target. With so much energy working against her plan, she's not going to chance taking it out on you. If she tries to do it in secret, such as on the Internet, you'll all know it's her anyway. She can't hurt you. Her power is false. If she does manage to get a dig in, remember this: "If with heart and soul you're doing good, do you think you can be stopped? Even if you suffer for it, you're still better off" (1 Peter 3:13, *The Message*).

> I don't like to admit this now, but last year I WAS a bully. It was because my parents were splitting up and I was so angry I just took it out on girls I knew wouldn't fight back. So if somebody's being mean to you, it's usually because she's insecure. She's probably weaker than you, just so you know.

## How to make it official:

If you and your friends really want to make wiping out bullying your mission:

- ○ Write a pledge that anyone can take who wants to join you.

- ○ Ask your principal (or whoever's in charge) if you can post it in your school, co-op, dance studio, or wherever meanness is happening.

It's super effective if you have people sign it and display it with the signatures. Anyone looking at that will know she doesn't have a chance of getting away with bullying.

# SAMPLE PLEDGE

I, _____, pledge
to be a part of making this a safe place for EVERYONE by:

○ refusing to put labels on people.

○ never passing on rumors.

○ not laughing at put-down jokes.

○ calling people on their mean behavior.

○ standing up for victims.

○ helping victims stand up for themselves.

○ reporting bullying to adults when necessary.

○ respecting every person's right to be herself.

Signatures:_____

_____

_____

_____

You're not forming an alliance *against* any person. You're forming one *for* a world that is safe and accepting— where people can be who they are. You can be part of the generation that stops the hate. How does that sound?

## Just So You Know

In 2011, 5.7 MILLION kids and teens were bullied, were bullies, or both. You can be part of bringing that down to ZERO.

## That Is SO Me

Put a star beside each action you think you could take. You probably won't star all of them because different people are good at different things. Don't be afraid to imagine yourself a little out of your comfort zone though.

I think I could ...

○ say hi to a girl other people are mean to.

○ invite a girl who gets picked on in the cafeteria to sit with me at lunch.

○ tell a bully she has no right to keep a girl from having peace at school.

○ start a group whose mission is to stop the bullying.

○ join an anti-bullying group.

○ sign an anti-bullying pledge.

○ make a pledge with my best friend or group of

friends not to gossip, spread rumors, use labels, or laugh at put-down jokes.

○ walk with a girl so she can go where she needs to in school.

○ be part of a group that shields a girl from bullies who block her path.

○ encourage a bullied girl to talk to a trusted adult or even go with her.

○ use my blog or online journal to spread good news instead of bad.

○ use my blog or online journal to speak out against bullying without mentioning any names.

○ apologize to a bullied girl I didn't help when she needed it.

○ pray for the bullies and the bullied alike, as well as for courage for me to stand up for what's right.

Choose one of the things you starred, and JUST DO IT! When you do:

○ Start small.

○ Then do something bigger.

○ Don't try to do it all at once.

Do what you can, and you'll be able to do more.
Every step you take will make a difference.

## YOU CAN DO IT

Do I even have to tell you what *this* section is going to be about? I hope you're fired up!

## What you'll need:

- ⭘ a Bible for each person
- ⭘ this book
- ⭘ your BBB
- ⭘ those wonderful art supplies
- ⭘ snacks

## What you're doing:

You're taking the first steps toward being the whole generation that no longer says, "Bullying is just what kids do." So go ahead and create a new page for your BBB called "No More Innocent Bystanders!" Make it look bold because it is. With that done, you're ready to move on.

## How to make it happen:

Together create a pledge like the one on page 192. Do a "rough draft" first because you might want to add to it in the next step.

Turn to what we call the Sermon on the Mount (because Jesus preached it on a mountain), Matthew 5:1–7:27.

Find at least five things Jesus says to do that will make you a good friend—not only to people you like, but also to the world. Write them in your own words and, if it seems right, add them to your pledge. This activity will teach you that it is not just "nice" if you treat people well, it's *required* of a follower of Christ! But it also shows you exactly HOW to do it, and ya gotta love that.

Example:

"Love your enemies and pray for those who persecute you" (Matthew 5:44).

Add to the pledge: *Pray for bullies, and don't try to get back at them.*

Now make a beautiful copy of the pledge for your BBB. Both/all/you should sign it, naturally.

If the time is right, make a larger and equally gorgeous copy of your pledge and take it to an adult you trust to stand behind you. Together, discuss whether it's appropriate to get more signatures and post that pledge in a place where it can serve as the first step toward making your world bully-free. Just the way God wants it.

# That's What I'm Talkin' About

In the days ahead, write, draw, or doodle your responses to what happens with your friends.

I would say our pledge is _____

_____

_____ .

Now when we see bullying going on we _____

_____

_____ .

I know it's making a difference (or didn't make a difference)

because _____

_____

_____ .

The adult we talked to _____

_____

_____ .

# 7

# Best Friends for Life

Nicole isn't a mini-woman anymore. She's thirteen now. But when she "graduated" from the tween blog to the teen blog, she sent me this e-mail, and I've been saving it to share with you. She says:

"The whole time I was a tween, starting from like age nine, the friend thing was so confusing. I'd have a best friend for, like, a month, and then one of us would get mad and we'd 'break up.' Sometimes a third friend would join in and then they'd start ignoring me. Once I was even bullied by two girls who had promised they were going to be in my WEDDING someday (LOL). I guess I always had friends, but it didn't seem like I could trust any of them.

"Then we did the series on friends on the tween blog, and I finally started to get it. I figured out that it wasn't always somebody else's fault when things went wrong. And I quit running away crying every time somebody hurt my feelings. And then like two months later, I realized I had this great group of friends—four of us—and we were actually NICE to each other!

"Three of us are still friends (one moved away), and I think that's because of a combination of all the things I practiced from our series and me getting closer to God and just becoming more mature.

"So I just want to say to the tweens on your blog to listen to good advice and take everything to the Lord and don't think it's always going to be so hard because it isn't. I wish I had just had more fun with my friends instead of worrying so much, and I hope they can do that now."

I don't think Nicole can recite all the "advice" I gave in that series, but I bet she could tell you what I'm about to tell you as my parting words. Or, well, what *God's* about to tell you.

## GOT GOD?

You've read a lot of Scripture in this book, and you've even discovered some for yourself. Your mind is probably like a racetrack with all those verses tearing around in there. Jesus knew it was hard to keep it all straight, which is why he gave us a summary of the Law. He boiled it all down to just a few things we absolutely have to do in order to be the kind of friends God wants us to be.

> "Love the Lord your God with all your heart and with all your soul and with all your mind and with all your strength." The second is this: "Love your neighbor as yourself." There is no commandment greater than these.
>
> Mark 12:30–31

If at any time you face a girl politics problem and you can't remember the suggestions for it in this book, just do this: LOVE WITH EVERYTHING YOU HAVE.

That's what God does. That's what Jesus showed us to do. He said to think about how you want other people to treat you, and treat them that way.

If a friend is careless with your feelings, love her enough to tell her how you feel. Wouldn't you want her to tell you if it were the other way around?

If a girl looks lonely, love her enough to ask her how she's doing. Wouldn't you want somebody to do that to you if you were alone?

If somebody bullies you, love her enough not to spit right back in her face. Wouldn't you want somebody to control herself if you had a bully moment?

If you see somebody having a hard time with a Really Mean Girl, love her enough to stand up for her. Wouldn't you be just so grateful if someone saved you from humiliation?

If bullying becomes a problem at your school, love your generation enough to do what you can to stop it. Don't you want somebody to make your school a safe place to be?

> You can't go wrong when you love others. When you add up everything in the law code, the sum total is love.
>
> Romans 13:10 (The Message)

## Who, ME?

Fill in the blank:

I wish somebody would _____ for me.

Now, how ya gonna do that for somebody else?

_____

_____

_____

And don't forget that although Jesus isn't physically in your classroom when the teacher says to pick a partner for a project or in the locker room when you're changing for PE and some girl says, "When are you going to grow some breasts?" he's there inside you, whispering that you have a friend in him. Okay, no, you can't tell your teacher Jesus is going to work with you on your science project, or you can't expect him to materialize and stand between you and that potty-mouthed girl. But I'm going to let Hope tell you how that **does** work.

"I was left out a lot," she wrote to me, "and when I did find a really good friend, she suddenly had to move away. My heart broke into a million pieces as well as any hopes I had of ever making another friend. I was once again friendless, lonely, and sad.

"I guess because I didn't have any other choice, I started thinking about our pastor always saying that Jesus is our friend. I started talking to him in my prayers that way and imagining it when I read the Bible, and pretty soon I started feeling like he was really there. He became the BEST friend I EVER had! He was ALWAYS there even when nobody else was. Is that awesome or what? And the best part is that I didn't find him. He found me."

Need I say more?

## HERE'S THE DEAL

Before you go on to loving everyone from your BFF to the local RMG, don't forget that there are three parts in the summary of the Law:

- Love God.

- Love your neighbor.

- Love *yourself.*

Let's take an important look at that third one. The commandment says to love your neighbor the same way you love yourself.

> ❝Isn't it conceited to love yourself? It sounds like you're a snob or something!❞

Really? Think about this. If the way you treat *yourself* is to …

- put yourself down,

- force yourself to do things you don't really want to do,

- let yourself be ridiculed and not do anything to stop it,

then possibly without even realizing it, you might very well treat your neighbor the same way. Yeah. Think about it.

## Who, ME?

I don't treat myself very well when I ...

_____

_____

_____

_____

_____

Loving yourself is NOT

- always putting yourself first.

- always trying to get your own way.

- telling everyone how fabulous you are all the time.

## Just So You Know

The more you say a thing about yourself, the more likely you are to believe it.

That includes:

- "I'm fat."

- "No one will ever like me."

- "I'm a math moron."

Loving yourself IS

- taking good care of the beautiful true self God made.

- never letting anyone take away your power to be that beautiful self.

Your true self comes through when these things happen:

- You do the things you really love to do, whether anyone else loves to do them or not.

- You are comfortable with people, not worrying about how you look or what you're going to say.

- You're honest with your friends.

- You can hurt, either for yourself or for someone else.

- You do something unselfish for someone and don't go, "Did you see me do that?"

- You pray without "performing" for God.

- A feeling of joy bubbles up inside you.

- You truly like who you are.

*That's* the YOU that you need to love so you can shine love on everyone else.

## Who, ME?

Write down one small but nice thing you can do for yourself today.

_____

_____

_____

_____

_____

(Then do it!)

## What loving yourself LOOKS like:

You make your own decisions about who you're going to be friends with.

You choose friends who like you just as you truly are, who you never have to be anything more for, even if that means you only have one close friend.

You don't let anyone pressure you into doing or saying anything you know isn't right.

You give up something of your own if someone else truly needs it, including your place in the spotlight.

❝ When you say, 'It is important to love yourself,' I think about how I used to not know who I was and what God's purpose was for me. I acted really hyper around a lot of my friends, but that wasn't the real me, and I didn't love that 'me.' Once I realized that I am uniquely me and that God placed talents, unique attributes, and gifts inside of me, I began to become the most beautiful me I could ever be. :-) ❞

When you love your neighbor as yourself, you never give up who you really are, because no one else ever really needs for you to do that. This is what it might look like when you love your neighbor as yourself without giving up who you are:

- Your BFF didn't get her homework done and she asks if she can copy yours. You say no, but that you'll help her do her own before it's time to turn it in.

- Your group of friends wants to send a prank e-mail, and you're the only one with her own computer in her room. You say you will absolutely not participate in that, and you don't think they should either.

- A friend begs you not to tell anyone that her stepfather is hitting her hard enough to leave bruises. You say she needs help from a grown-up, and you will go with her to get it—or you will tell an adult yourself.

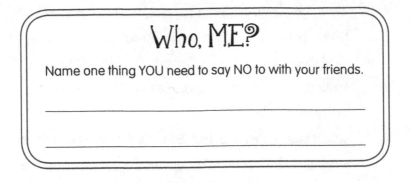

## Who, ME?

Name one thing YOU need to say NO to with your friends.

_____

_____

Most important, when you make a mistake—and you will because you are a human being—

- ask God to forgive you,

- ask your friend to forgive you,

- and get yourself to forgive you too.

Then keep on growing into the best friend you can possibly be.

## That Is SO Me

Here is a list of the main things you've read about in this book. Put a star next to any that you would like to work on in your friend world.

○ Having sister chicks instead of a closed clique (chapter 2)

○ Handling friendship flubs in my group of buds (chapter 3)

○ Making new friends (chapter 4)

○ Dealing with people who bully me OR changing my bullying behavior (chapter 5)

○ Putting a stop to bullying, period (chapter 6)

○ Being a good friend to myself (chapter 7)

If you have only one star, put a number 1 next to it. If you starred more than one thing, number those items, with 1 being the most important to you and 2 the next most important, 3 the next, and so on.

If you had NO stars, be available to other girls who are working on things, but remember there are always ways to be better.

## One more thing:

Enjoy this work of being in a relationship. For all their griping, the psalm writers did.

> These God-chosen lives all around—what splendid friends they make!
>
> Psalm 16:3 (The Message)

Go now, and love those splendid friends!

## YOU CAN DO IT

You've worked hard in this book, right? Now it's time to celebrate!

## What you'll need:

○ Your BBB

Before you meet, ask each girl to bring something that shows how much she loves her friends (or you, if there are just two of you). It should be something that can be put into the BBB, and if each person is doing one, each girl should bring one for everybody. It can be a special card, words to a song, a drawing, a poem she's written, maybe a Bible verse for each person. Tell your buds they can be creative. Anything goes, as long as it's loving.

○ Those ever-present art supplies

○ Each person brings a snack treat she knows the rest of the group will love (because she knows you that well now).

## What you're doing:

You're finding out some really important stuff:

- How much you have to be thankful for.

- How important you are to each other.

- How much you know about each other.

- What you have that you can share with girls who aren't as blessed as you are right now.

- That no matter what flubs and other issues you may have to work on, you are a pretty spectacular friend already.

## How to make it happen:

Give each person a chance to share what she's brought. Take your time appreciating each thing.

Talk, giggle, hug—maybe even cry happy tears. Treasure the love in the room.

Make a new section for the BBB called "Treasures."

Paste in the new gifts.

Make room for more pages for the future—because the friendship fun has only begun!!!

# That's What I'm Talkin' About

When the party's over and you have some quiet time, fill in these blanks or write more or doodle or draw or just dream about:

I know Jesus is my friend because _____

_____

_____

I'm my own friend when_____

_____

_____

I love my friends so much I want to _____

_____

_____

Love one another the way I loved you. This is the very best way to love.

John 15:12 (The Message)

## Faithgirlz Journal

### My Doodles, Dreams and Devotion

Looking for a place to dream, doodle, and record your innermost questions and secrets? You will find what you seek within the pages of the Faithgirlz Journal, which has plenty of space for you to discover who you are, explore who God is shaping you to be, or write down whatever inspires you. Each journal page has awesome quotes and powerful Bible verses to encourage you on your walk with God! So grab a pen, colored pencils, or even a handful of markers. Whatever you write is just between you and God.

*Available in stores and online!*

# NIV Faithgirlz! Bible, Revised Edition

*Nancy Rue*

Every girl wants to know she's totally unique and special. This Bible says that with Faithgirlz! sparkle. Through the many in-text features found only in the Faithgirlz! Bible, girls will grow closer to God as they discover the journey of a lifetime.

Features include:

- Book introductions—Read about the who, when, where, and what of each book.

- Dream Girl—Use your imagination to put yourself in the story.

- Bring It On!—Take quizzes to really get to know yourself.

- Is There a Little (Eve, Ruth, Isaiah) in You?—See for yourself what you have in common.

- Words to Live By—Check out these Bible verses that are great for memorizing.

- What Happens Next?—Create a list of events to tell a Bible story in your own words.

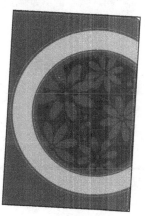

- Oh, I Get It!—Find answers to Bible questions you've wondered about.

- The complete NIV translation

- Features written by bestselling author Nancy Rue

*Available in stores and online!*

# Talk It Up!

*Want free books?*
*First looks at the best new fiction?*
*Awesome exclusive merchandise?*

We want to hear from you!

Give us your opinions on titles, covers, and stories.
Join the Z Street Team.

Email us at zstreetteam@zondervan.com
to sign up today!

Also—Friend us on Facebook!

www.facebook.com/goodteenreads

- Video Trailers
- Connect with your favorite authors
- Sneak peeks at new releases
- Giveaways
- Fun discussions
- And much more!